THE PARABLE OF THE

FIG TREE

THE PARABLE OF THE

FIG TREE

Discerning the Signs that Herald Christ's Return

By Ryan Habbena

Strong Tower Publishing

Bellefonte, PA

www.strongtowerpublishing.com

ISBN 0981527647

LCCN: 2009933844

Cover design: Nick Coldagelli

Illustrations: Jenny Habbena

Unless otherwise indicated, all Scripture quotations, unless otherwise indicated, taken from the NEW AMERICAN STANDARD BIBLE®, copyright © 1960, 1962, 1963, 1968, 1971, 1972, 1973, 1975, 1977, 1995 by The Lockman Foundation. Used by permission.

TABLE OF CONTENTS

TABLE OF GRAPHICS

1

THE PARABLE
OF THE FIG TREE

Discerning the Signs that Herald Christ's Return

In the second chapter of the book of Ezekiel, we read a sobering exhortation:

> "Son of man, I have appointed you a watchman to the house of Israel; whenever you hear a word from My mouth, warn them from Me. When I say to the wicked, 'You will surely die,' and you do not warn him or speak out to warn the wicked from his wicked way that he may live, that wicked man shall die in his iniquity, but his blood I will require at your hand." (Eze. 2:17–18)

This was the message delivered to the prophet Ezekiel. He was accountable before God to announce the reality of coming judgment. He was appointed to

1

be a watchman to the house of Israel. A watchman in Ezekiel's time was one who was placed at his post to watch over the city walls. If threats, harm, or destruction were on the horizon, he was to sound the alarm. This text holds an implication that resounds for the church of Jesus Christ. The faith delivered once and for all has been entrusted to the saints. The King, who endured the cross for the sins of the world and was raised from the dead forevermore, is *returning*. When He returns, He will be not be redeeming the world through suffering, but "dealing out retribution to those who do not know God and to those who do not obey the gospel of our Lord Jesus" (2 Thess. 1:8). Judgment is approaching on the horizon of human history. Much of the church is either sleeping at their posts or falsely sounding the alarm.

CRYING WOLF

Most of us were brought up hearing Aesop's fables. These fables, or short stories, were penned and passed on to demonstrate certain moral or enduring truths. One of the more famous fables is "The Boy Who Cried Wolf." According to the story, a certain shepherd boy became bored tending his sheep, and thus he found it amusing to cry "Wolf!" In response, the villagers would race to the boy's side, only to find him amused by the false alarm to which they had fallen prey. While he continued to amuse himself by repeating this alarm, the day came when the wolf actually arrived. Once again, the shepherd boy sounded the alarm, but this time, the villagers didn't believe him. No one came, and the wolf proceeded to make a tidy meal of the boy's flock.

Over the last two thousand years, many have cried "wolf" regarding the second coming of Jesus Christ. Church history is peppered with prognostications and announcements of when the King will return. Many have cried, "Here comes the Christ!" but the King has not returned. While many have sounded the alarm in error, the truth is still this: One day the events of the end of the age will *actually* begin to unfold. With deception surrounding us and so many false prophets scattered throughout the land, how are we to discern the true signs of Christ's return from the false? Our Lord has not left us without a witness. We have His Word, preserved through the ages, to guide, protect, and prepare us.

LEARN THE PARABLE OF THE FIG TREE

Our King left us clear instructions regarding the end of the age. We are not to be taken off guard because He "told us everything in advance" (Matt. 24:24). He exhorted all of His disciples to learn the parable of the fig tree. Through learning this parable, not only are we equipped with the true knowledge of what will transpire, but we are able to discern and reject the false prophecies that continually arise.

Allow me to paint the context in which the parable of the fig tree was proclaimed. During the last week of His earthly ministry, the Lord arrived at the temple and announced powerful woes upon

Jerusalem's leadership. Because of their unwillingness to gather under the Messiah, the Lord declared: "From now on you will not see Me until you say, 'Blessed is he who comes in the name of the Lord!'" (Matt. 23:39).

Jesus' disciples heard their Master speak of the destruction of the temple and that there would be a delay before He would "come again" to Israel.[1] Their expectations were high. This language would have roused expectations of the restoration of Israel, so the disciples sought answers. The scene was as follows: "As Jesus was sitting on the Mount of Olives, the disciples came to him privately and asked, 'Tell us when will these things be? And what will be the sign of your coming, and the end of the age?'" (Matt. 24:3–4). The disciples understood that the Lord would "come" and that this would mean "the end of the age." The Greek word for "coming" is *parousia*. This term was often used for the arrival and presence of royalty. Jesus' coming as the conquering King would usher in the end of the age. The expectation in the first century was intense. The disciples would have understood the end of the age as referring to the end of Gentile domination leading to the fulfillment of God's promises to Israel. The end of the age would usher in Israel's King, who would judge the nations and reign over all the earth in justice and righteousness. Thus, Jesus accepted their questions and proceeded to reveal the events and conditions that would lead to the consummation of human history.

After beginning His discourse by warning, "See to it that no one deceives you" (24:4), the Lord proceeded to give a detailed outline of the events and conditions leading to the end of the age. This is known as the Olivet Discourse. Event after event was prophesied by the King, culminating with His return in glory. Then the Lord commanded His disciples to learn the all-important parable:

> "Now learn the parable from the fig tree: when its branch has already become tender and puts forth its leaves, you know that summer is near; so, you too, when you see all these things, recognize that He is near, right at the door." (Matt. 24:32–33)

The central goal of this book is for the reader to become well acquainted with this parable. The Greek verb is imperative: "learn" (*mathete*). This is a command. Our Lord exhorts us to learn this parable. If we see that which He outlined, we are to recognize that He is near. This particular parable is both simple and profound.

A SIMPLE AND PROFOUND PARABLE

The parable of the fig tree is simple in that its meaning is straight-forward. We are to look at the fig tree. The fig tree is barren in wintertime. Yet when the "branch becomes tender," which means that it is beginning to bud, we know the season of summer is near. In the same manner, when one sees "all these things" that Jesus outlined in His Olivet Discourse, one is to discern that His coming is near, even "right at the door."[2]

Though understanding this parable is simple on one level, it is deeply profound on another. I consider the Olivet Discourse to be the heart of understanding the second coming and the events that surround it. The discourse points back to important passages in the Old Testament, but also becomes the source for continued end-times teaching in the New Testament. In a sense, the Olivet Discourse is the glue that holds the whole prophetic framework together. As we progress through this book, we will see how, in His discourse, the Lord alludes to the prophets of Daniel and Joel. We will see how His teaching becomes the source of Paul's instruction in the Thessalonian epistles. We will reach forward to the book of Revelation and see how the discourse provides the framework through which we understand the Apocalypse of John.

My aim is to accurately expound the essential end-times texts and highlight the biblical links that the Lord left for us, enabling us to better perceive the whole picture. This, of course, does not mean that every detail is plain and clear. Far from it. But it is my conviction that the general picture has been sufficiently laid out and that the diligent student of the scriptures can grasp the essentials of end-times prophecy.

A MOST IMPORTANT STARTING POINT

End-times discussion can be fascinating. Peering into the Word of God and marveling at how God plans to consummate His purposes and promises is a soul-stirring endeavor. The return of Jesus Christ is a settled fact. It is history that is yet to transpire. Yet, it is of utmost importance that we realize why this day has not yet occurred. Although nearly two-thousand years have passed since Jesus promised to return, the delay is for salvation.

The apostle Peter teaches us the following:

> "But by His word the present heavens and earth are being reserved for fire, kept for the day of judgment and destruction of ungodly men. But do not let this one fact escape your notice, beloved, that with the Lord one day is like a thousand years, and a thousand years like one day. The Lord is not slow about His promise, as some count slowness, but is patient toward you, not wishing for any to perish but for all to come to repentance." (2 Pet. 3:7–9)

The coming wrath of God is hanging over humanity because of sin. Since the beginning, we have deliberately and continually broken His law and refused His mercy. But our gracious God is patient toward us. His plans and purposes will be established. He is gathering His people from every tribe, nation, and tongue. He is doing so through the good news.

The good news is this: Even though we were dead in trespasses and sin, God sent His Son to remedy the situation. Just as He promised, when the fullness of time came, God sent forth His Son born of a woman, born under the Law, to redeem us. Although existing as God and with God for all eternity, Jesus was born of a young virgin. The Lord of Hosts arrived in humble circumstances: as a baby, laid in an animal trough. His small newborn hands were destined to be pierced. They were also destined to hold the scepter of the unshakable kingdom of God.

Jesus was the spotless Lamb of God, sent to take away the sin of the world. He was, and is, pure. No sin or deceit can be found in Him. He lived a sinless life to serve as the perfect substitute—to trade His righteousness for our wretchedness. This transaction took place on the cross of Calvary, where He was crucified for our transgressions. As He breathed the last breaths of His earthly mission, He announced the victory: "It is finished."

Death could not hold Him. He rose from the dead three days later, and He subsequently announced to His disciple John, "I am alive forevermore!" (Rev. 1:10). He ascended to the right hand of the Father and now the whole world awaits His return in glory.

So what is the appropriate, God-prescribed response to this good news? We are called to *repent and believe*. We are to repent in turning away from sin, self, and Satan. We are to believe by trusting in the person and work of Jesus Christ. When one believes in the King, he or she becomes a child of God, who will always preserve His children. If you have not trusted in Jesus Christ, this message has met you by divine appointment. Repent and believe, for the kingdom of God is at hand! All who believe have been given an eager expectation from the graceful hand of God: We "wait for His Son from heaven, whom He raised from the dead, that is Jesus, who rescues us from the wrath to come" (1 Thess. 1:10).

ESTABLISHING A FRAMEWORK OF INTERPRETATION

While we wait, we have been given exhortations in regards to this "great expectation." It is imperative when studying the scriptures to fix important precepts to form our framework of interpretation. We must apply the principles of sound biblical interpretation. The scriptures have numerous implications and applications, but only one meaning. This meaning is determined by the author and is discovered through careful consideration of the historical, literary, and biblical context of the passage. This takes time and diligence, but it is essential to both our task as interpreters of scripture and faithfulness to its author. Our calling is clear:

> Be diligent to present yourself approved to God as a workman who does not need to be ashamed, accurately handling the word of truth. (2 Tim. 2:15)

As we engage in the task of interpretation, while reading expositional work and considering theological arguments (including mine), we all should ask ourselves the following questions: "Is this an interpretation based on sound exposition? Is this the most compelling interpretation based on the immediate context and the whole counsel of God? Am I bringing traditions to the text that may be preventing me from a proper understanding? Are my emotions preventing the truth from piercing my conscience?"

This is just a sampling of the self-examination we should undertake when engaging the scriptures. Allowing our traditions and presuppositions to be challenged by the Word of God is how our minds become renewed. When truth captivates the conscience, we must be willing to leave all previous beliefs behind. For some, this process may be costly, but it is not an option.

During any open and thorough study of the scriptures, traditions may be challenged. Emotional ties may be tested. Long-held arguments and systems may be taken to the biblical test. My earnest prayer is that, through reading this book, you will both understand the commands of our glorious King regarding the end of the age and proceed to prepare properly.

TAKE HEED

Exhortations relating to the end of the age are not trivial matters. These instructions have been delivered to us with the utmost seriousness by the Lord Jesus and His commissioned apostles. The deception that surrounds us is ever growing and will one day be unleashed like never before. Wolves will arrive, seeking to prey on the Lord's flock. Therefore, we must "read and heed" the God-breathed knowledge and wisdom preserved for us:

> "Let no one in any way deceive you." (2 Thess. 2:3)
>
> "See to it that no one misleads you." (Matt. 24:4)
>
> "But take heed; behold, I have told you everything in advance." (Mark 13:23)
>
> "What I say to you I say to all: Be on the alert." (Mark 13:37)

During His first coming, Jesus admonished His contemporaries regarding their failure to recognize the hour of their visitation.

> "When it is evening, you say, 'It will be fair weather, for the sky is red.' And in the morning, 'There will be a storm today, for the sky is red and threatening.' Do you know how to discern the appearance of the sky, but cannot discern the signs of the times?" (Matt. 16:2–3)

Storm clouds are gathering on the horizon of human history. The world is unaware, and much of the church is asleep. With such serious exhortations fueling us, may we proceed to learn the parable of the fig tree and, thus, be prepared and eagerly watching for the return of the King of Kings.

11

End Notes 1

[1] The narrative indicates that Jesus is speaking of the destruction of the temple and that the "delay" implied in 23:39 was what prompted their questions. These matters stirred the expectations of the disciples. Jesus' teaching throughout Matthew 24–25 serves to both answer their questions and correct their misunderstandings.

[2] Many interpreters have viewed this parable as speaking of Israel, since the fig tree often represented Israel. However, the text itself speaks of "all these things" as the referent of the budding tree. Luke's account further generalizes this parable beyond the fig tree to "all the trees" (Luke 21), which indicates that it is the budding that is important. Therefore, to learn the parable of the fig tree, we are to be on the alert for all the events and conditions our Lord outlines in the Olivet Discourse so that we may discern the season of His return.

2

A COMMAND

FROM THE KING

Is the Parable of the Fig Tree for Me to Learn and Apply?

"Therefore everyone who hears these words of Mine and acts on them, may be compared to a wise man who built his house on the rock. And the rain fell, and the floods came, and the winds blew and slammed against that house; and yet it did not fall, for it had been founded on the rock. Everyone who hears these words of Mine and does not act on them, will be like a foolish man who built his house on the sand. The rain fell, and the floods came, and the winds blew and slammed against that house; and it fell—and great was its fall." (Matt. 7:24–27)

These are the words Jesus gave His listeners in the wake of the Sermon on the Mount. The words of Christ are the words of life. We are called to carefully listen, learn, and apply His teaching. Those who hear these words and put them into practice build their houses on the rock. Those who don't will experience ruin. Since acting on His words is so important, before expounding the specifics of the parable of the fig tree, we must have a satisfactory answer to this question: To whom were the words of the Olivet Discourse spoken? Are they for believers of today? When Jesus instructs, "When you see all these things recognize that He is near, right at the door," does this apply to believers of today? Are we to be looking for "all these things"? Or does this apply to another group of believers?

There are two primary challenges to the contemporary application of the Olivet Discourse to the church. Ironically, these two challenges come from opposite ends of the eschatological spectrum. One is *preterism*. The other is *pretribulationalism*. Both of these schools of thought have large followings. Though vastly different in their interpretations of the Olivet Discourse, they have a common denominator. Both believe that the Olivet Discourse does not carry direct application to contemporary believers. First I will briefly explain these two views of the Olivet Discourse. Then I will engage each position by offering biblical reasons why their interpretations miss the mark and why the parable of the fig tree indeed applies to us today.

THE CHALLENGE OF PRETERISM

On one end of the interpretive spectrum is preterism. In the wake of the turn of the millennium, this particular understanding of the end times has experienced a wide resurgence. The central belief of preterism is that the Olivet Discourse and the book of Revelation had their primary fulfillment in the destruction of the temple and Jerusalem in A.D. 70. For this reason, preterism argues that Jesus' commands in the context of the Olivet Discourse (including the parable of the fig tree) were intended for the generation that experienced the destruction of Jerusalem. Note Gary Demar's comments regarding this parable.

> Jesus used the parable of the fig tree as an analogy. His point was that when leaves begin to sprout on a fig tree—or, for that matter, on "all the trees" (Luke 21:29)—it is a sign that summer is near. In a similar way, when Jesus' first-century audience saw certain signs, they knew Jesus was near, "right at the door." Near to what? Near to fulfilling the promise He made about coming within a generation to destroy the temple. This is the simple and clear meaning of the text. Any other interpretation wildly stretches the Bible beyond its intended meaning.[1]

While preterism has a variety of sub-positions, this quote well represents the central and most commonly held teaching of preterism as it relates to the Olivet Discourse.

We can then see why preterists do not see the parable of the fig tree as having a direct, contemporary application to believers. Since, by definition, "all these things" that Jesus describes in the parable of the fig tree constitute what transpired leading up to A.D. 70, then the command to learn the parable would not apply after the events transpired. Therefore, the preterist view of the Olivet Discourse holds that the current believer *cannot* read and put into practice watching for "all the things" since it is impossible to watch for events that have already taken place.

THE CHALLENGE OF PRETRIBULATIONALISM

Pretribulationalism strikingly differs from preterism in that it affirms the futurity of Olivet Discourse (in other words, it holds that the events Jesus outlines in Matthew 24 have yet to occur). While vastly different in its interpretation, pretribulationalism also holds to the position that the Olivet Discourse does not have direct application to contemporary believers. Why? Because it teaches that "all of these things" will occur within a seven-year "tribulation" period and that the rapture (the raising and gathering of God's elect) will occur before this takes place. Since the church will be raptured before the "tribulation," contemporary believers will not be here for these events when they occur. Therefore, as in preterism, the commands to learn the parable and to recognize that He is near by seeing these signs do not apply to us. Instead, they apply to either Jewish believers or "tribulation saints" who come to faith during the "time of tribulation" after the rapture.

John MacArthur, a man I hold in high regard and from whom have learned much regarding the Bible and ministry, holds to the pretribulational position. He has this to say about the parable of the fig tree and the Olivet Discourse:

> The point of the parable is utterly uncomplicated; even a child can tell by looking at a fig tree that summer is near. Likewise, the generation that sees *all* these signs come to pass will know with certainty that Christ's return is near . . . Those who recognize the signs will realize that Christ's coming is at the door. Those who live during the Tribulation can have absolute confidence that He will return soon, despite the viciousness of the persecutions, no matter how convincing the lies of the deceivers, regardless of how much it seems Satan, not God, is in control of these things. In Christ's own words, "See, I have told you beforehand" (Matt. 24:25).[2]

MacArthur's exposition is sound regarding the central point of the parable of the fig tree, yet he does not hold that the command to watch for these signs could apply to the contemporary church. This is only

for those "who live during the Tribulation."
MacArthur, thus, asks the question: "Where is the
church during the Tribulation?" He answers:

> [T]he entire church will be removed from
> the earth before the Tribulation begins.
> Scripture indicates that during Daniel's
> seventieth week, national Israel, not the
> church, will be the focus of God's earthly
> program . . . The Rapture is indeed
> imminent; it could occur at any time. The
> second stage of Christ's return—His
> coming in glory *with* the saints—is the
> event all the signs and warnings in the
> Olivet Discourse point to.[3]

Therefore, MacArthur sees the "watch"
warnings of the Olivet Discourse as applying to
"Tribulation" saints and not for us, the church. Since
this is so, these signs are not anything we need to be
immediately concerned with.[4] (The issue of
"imminence" that MacArthur mentioned will be
addressed in chapter ten).

While these two views of the Olivet Discourse
(preterism and pretribulationalism) are on opposite
ends of the interpretive spectrum, they hold a very
important commonality. Both hold that the Olivet
Discourse, and thus the need to learn and apply the
parable of the fig tree, do not directly apply to
contemporary believers. Preterists believe this parable
was for the generation that saw the destruction of
Jerusalem and that its application ends there.
Pretribulationalists believe this parable is for Jewish

believers, or "Tribulation saints" who come to faith during the "Tribulation period" after the church is raptured, and therefore the warnings of this parable do not directly apply to us. They are not for us to specifically learn and apply.

On the contrary, not only do I believe that the parable of the fig tree *is* for us to learn and apply, I believe it is of great importance that we put Jesus' words into practice. The many reasons for this will be explained throughout this book.

First, however, we need to establish that these words are for *us* to read and heed. There is no need to parse the above views and interact with them separately, as the reasons offered below will answer both views. Allow me to outline three prime reasons the Olivet Discourse applies to us and thus the parable of the fig tree is for all the church to learn and apply.

REASON #1: THE GREAT COMMISSION AND THE CONSTRUCTION OF MATTHEW

The book of Matthew is the glorious proclamation that Jesus is the fulfillment of the promises given to Abraham and David. He is the "son of David" and the "son of Abraham" (Matt. 1:1). He is the eternal King who brings the blessing of the gospel to all the nations (Matt. 28:18–20). While this is the strand upon which Matthew pens his gospel, the book is also well viewed as a handbook of discipleship. Handbooks of discipleship apply to all believers, not just a select few at a specific time in history.

A close reading of the text reveals that Matthew's narrative of the life of Christ is interspersed with discourses instructing believers in His revolutionary, authoritative teachings. In progressing through the gospel, we see challenges to read and heed the instructions of Christ. As the gospel comes to its conclusion, we are presented with what is known as the Great Commission. Many have seen this as a simple call to evangelism. While this is a prime element of this significant text, its meaning goes further.

> And Jesus came up and spoke to them, saying, "All authority has been given to Me in heaven and on earth. Go therefore and make disciples of all the nations, baptizing them in the name of the Father and the Son and the Holy Spirit, *teaching them to observe all that I commanded you*; and lo, I am with you always, even to the end of the age." (Matt. 28:18–20, emphasis added)

Those who carry the gospel of Jesus Christ are to instruct those who believe to "observe all that He commanded." Jesus instructed His disciples to pass on His instructions and gave them the authority to command all to observe His teachings. He is with those who take this message to the nations until the end of the age, a term that is a focal point of the Olivet Discourse.

As we consider Matthew's intent, we do well to reflect upon the teachings that Matthew has chronicled and intended for his readers to hear and obey. Matthew chronicled Jesus' teaching in the Sermon on the Mount, which forms the ethical basis of life in the New Covenant and reveals our need for a Savior (Matthew 5–7). He gave insight into the parables of the kingdom that reveal the nature of the kingdom of heaven and the proper response to the gospel (Matthew 13). He gave instructions to the church in dealing with offenses in the church and forgiveness (Matthew 18). Finally, He gave instructions regarding His second coming.

We are compelled to hear and obey the teaching of Jesus, including His instructions regarding the end of the age. Therefore, the content of Matthew and the power of the Great Commission compel us to learn and apply the parable of the fig tree.

Reason #2: The Teaching of the Thessalonian Epistles

The next reason that the parable of the fig tree is intended for us to learn and apply is the relationship between the Olivet Discourse and the Thessalonian epistles. Both of Paul's epistles have end-times events as a primary theme. First Thessalonians records the comforting teaching of the rapture of God's people and exhortations regarding the coming day of the Lord. Second Thessalonians gives us pertinent information regarding the sequence of end-times events, the reality of the coming "man of lawlessness," and the surety of his defeat by the King of Kings.

Parallels Between
The Olivet Discourse and the Thessalonians Epistles

•Both declare the "man of lawlessness" will be revealed when
he sets himself up in the temple
Matthew 24:15 - 2 Thessalonians 2:3-4
•Both describe lying signs and wonders that will characterize the time
immediately prior to Christ's return
Matthew 24:24 - 2 Thessalonians 2:9-10
•Both declare a great apostasy that precedes Christ's return
Matthew 24:10-12 - 2 Thessalonians 2:3
•Both describe the coming of the Lord and our being gathered to Him
Matthew 24:30-31 - 1 Thessalonians 4:13-17 - 2 Thessalonians 2:1
•Both declare the day of the Lord will come "like a thief" to unbelievers
Matthew 24:37-39, 43 - 1 Thessalonians 5:2-3
•Both exhort believers to "watch"
Matthew 24:42 - 1 Thessalonians 5:6
•Both declare the time of His coming is unknown
Matthew 24:36 - 1 Thessalonians 5:1

Most striking about the Thessalonian epistles is that the apostle Paul used the Olivet Discourse as his prime source of instruction and exhortation for the Thessalonian church about the times of the end. When trying to ascertain whether a biblical author is using a previous portion of scripture as a source, one looks for allusions. While usually a handful of allusions will well establish an author is drawing upon a previous portion of scripture, the Thessalonian epistles go well beyond this. These epistles are replete with allusions to the Olivet Discourse.[5] (Note the list in the graphic above as just a preview of the links we will explore throughout this book.)

Throughout this book, we will further explore the links between the Olivet Discourse and the Thessalonian epistles in both in language and content. The powerful points that Paul establishes within the framework of his epistles are the coming day of the Lord, the coming man of lawlessness, the coming apostasy, and the coming relief when Jesus returns in glory to resurrect His church, gather His elect, and deal out retribution to the wicked.

So how does this point speak to preterism, pretribulationalism, and the applicability of the events of the Olivet Discourse to the church? First, this point nullifies the preterist notion that the Olivet Discourse in its entirety is about the destruction of the temple in A.D. 70. Paul draws upon the Olivet Discourse to teach the church about the resurrection of the dead and His coming in glory to give relief to His people. The apostle writes in 1 Thessalonians 4:16–17 that at this time "the dead in Christ will rise first. Then we who are alive and remain will be caught up together with them." Since Paul sees the Olivet Discourse as within the timeframe of the resurrection of the dead, this supports the belief that the events of the Olivet Discourse are yet future. Secondly, this point nullifies the pretribulational notion that the Olivet Discourse is only for the Jews or "tribulation saints" and not for the church. Paul draws upon the Olivet Discourse to comfort the *church* and teach them about the sequence of end-times events. If Paul applied the Olivet Discourse to the church, then we are on solid footing when applying the commands of

Christ in the Olivet Discourse for the contemporary church to hear and observe, as well.

REASON #3: THE CONFIRMATION OF THE EARLY CHURCH

The eschatological views of the early church are an interesting and difficult study. Like us, the early church interacted with the scriptural texts and sought to understand them within their own context and therefore produced a variety of views regarding the end of the age. However, regarding those who were considered "orthodox," or faithful to central teachings of the apostles, they often held a view that mirrors the central view of this book. The early fathers frequently noted that the return of Christ will not occur until the markers Jesus outlined take place. As we will see, this is precisely the teaching of the Olivet Discourse and the parable of the fig tree.

Larry Crutchfield, who is a pretribulationalist and professor of early church history, while admitting pretribulationalism in its modern form is not found in the writings of the early church fathers, summarizes the view of the early fathers as "imminent intratribulationalism." Crutchfield writes:

> Even most of those who looked for Antichrist's appearance prior to the second advent, saw that event as occurring suddenly, and just as suddenly being followed by the rescue and rapture of the saints . . . This belief in the imminent

> return of Christ within the context of
> ongoing persecution has prompted us to
> broadly label the views of the earliest
> fathers: "imminent intratribulationism."[6]

In other words, many early church fathers wrote that it is in the midst of tribulation and persecution that the return of Christ is imminent (i.e. could occur at any moment). This precisely reflects what we read in the Olivet Discourse. This is precisely what Jesus teaches us with the parable of the fig tree. This is also precisely what this book seeks to demonstrate through exploring the scriptures in their respective contexts.

A good representation of the end-times teaching of the early church fathers is found in The Didache, or "the teaching of the twelve apostles." Although not part of scripture, it was a work often referenced or alluded to by this group of writers. This book is dated to the late first century or early second century. Consider the following excerpt:

> Watch for your life's sake. Let not your
> lamps be quenched, nor your loins
> unloosed; but be ye ready, for ye know not
> the hour in which our Lord cometh. But
> often shall ye come together, seeking the
> things which are befitting to your souls: for
> the whole time of your faith will not profit
> you, if ye be not made perfect in the last
> time. For in the last days false prophets
> and corrupters shall be multiplied, and the
> sheep shall be turned into wolves, and love

shall be turned into hate; for when lawlessness increaseth, they shall hate and persecute and betray one another, and then shall appear the world-deceiver as a son of God, and shall do signs and wonders, and the earth shall be delivered into his hands, and he shall do iniquitous things which have never yet come to pass since the beginning. Then shall the creation of men come into the fire of trial, and many shall be made to stumble and shall perish; but they that endure in their faith shall be saved from under the curse itself. And then shall appear the signs of the truth; first, the sign of an out-spreading in heaven; then the sign of the sound of the trumpet; and the third, the resurrection of the dead; yet not of all, but as it is said: The Lord shall come and all His saints with Him. Then shall the world see the Lord coming upon the clouds of heaven.

—The Didache (The Teaching of the Twelve Apostles) [100–120]

As you become acquainted with the parable of the fig tree, you will see that this section of The Didache drew heavily from the Olivet Discourse. Because this text was widely accepted for instruction in the early church after the destruction of the temple, it supports the contention that the early church fathers found continued application of the Olivet Discourse after A.D. 70 and that the Olivet Discourse

26

held instructions broadly applicable to the church of Jesus Christ.[7]

On their own, the views of the early church fathers do not prove or disprove that the Olivet Discourse describes yet-future events that are to be applied to the church. This must be established on scriptural grounds. But when combined with the first two points, which do just this, the views of the early church fathers provide additional confirmation that the Olivet Discourse, and thus the parable of the fig tree, are for us to learn and apply. Those in the earliest years, those closest to the time of the apostles, certainly did not believe that these instructions perished with the destruction of Jerusalem. Nor was there the notion that these applied only to a future group of people after the rapture of the church. Rather, as a reading of the early church fathers further confirms, the words of the Olivet Discourse are to be heeded, these events are to be watched for, and we are to be prepared.

IDENTIFYING "YOU"

Before we proceed to explore the specifics of the Olivet Discourse, a common question intrinsically related to our discussion needs a satisfactory answer: "Who is the 'you' that Christ addresses in the Olivet Discourse?" For instance, when Jesus begins His discourse, "See to it that no one misleads *you*," who is the "you" to whom He is speaking? Who is the "you" who is to hear and heed this message, as well as the rest of the commands in the Olivet Discourse?

On one level, we must affirm that this was addressed to the disciples who initially heard this message, the ones who asked the question in the first place. But as is the case with most of the instruction in the Gospels and Acts, the disciples were a part that represented the whole. The function of the Olivet Discourse is to put *all* believers in the war-time stance of watching. While only one group of believers will actually *experience* the events Jesus proclaims, every believer is called to be *able* to recognize the signs that He is near and *expect* His powerful return. Since all believers are called to be able to recognize the time of the end, we must proceed to hear the instructions Jesus gives for this unparalleled time. This preparation comes from learning the parable of the fig tree.

Samuel Tregelles, a nineteenth-century scholar who wrote extensively regarding the end times, taught of the necessity of watching for Jesus' coming through learning the parable of the fig tree:

> The coming spoken of is one as manifest as the lightning, as definite as the judgment of the flood. Its date is not revealed, so that it cannot be measured by years or centuries; but there are indications which will speak definitely to those who are truly watching. To this purpose the parable of the fig-tree was spoken, of which the application is, "So likewise ye, when ye shall see all these things, know that it is

nigh, even at the doors" (verse 33). It is to
persons thus instructed that the charge is
given to watch: they are not told to watch
irrespective of signals, but to be ready to
note them as they appear . . . To despise
the sign is to despise the Word of the Lord
who has promised it; it is to refuse
submission to His authority.[8]

The believer is to be ready through standing on
the gospel, hearing the words of Christ, and putting
them into practice. The parallel account of the Olivet
Discourse in Mark brings out this point clearly, when
at the culmination of the Discourse Mark chronicles
Jesus' call to be a believer who is obeying the Lord's
command:

"Watch therefore, for you do not know
when the master of the house is coming—
in the evening, at midnight, at the crowing
of the rooster, or in the morning—lest,
coming suddenly, he find you sleeping.
And what I say to *you*, I say to *all*: *Watch!*"
(Mark 13:35–37 NKJV, emphasis mine)

In light of these things, it is my contention that
the "you" in the Olivet Discourse has application on
three levels. First, the commands and instructions
were given to the initial disciples of Christ. Second,
they were passed on to be anticipated throughout the
whole era of the church. Third, they will find ultimate
fulfillment with the believers in Christ who actually
see all the events come to pass, culminating with the
return of Christ.

HOW ARE WE CALLED TO "OBSERVE" THE DISCOURSE?

Disciples of Christ are called to "observe all that He commanded." Since only one generation of believers will actually encounter the historical events prophesied, how are we called to observe these teachings? The time of the end will produce persecution against God's elect, diabolical deception, and the eventual furious wrath of Almighty God. In the Olivet Discourse, Christ has given the church as a whole a call to anticipation and preparation. Therefore, the Olivet Discourse is intended to be observed in the following manner: *Watch* for the signs that Jesus outlined. Then *read and heed* the preparatory exhortations of Christ, hiding them in our hearts until the time of the end.

This discourse should produce an *application of anticipation* for all who read and heed Christ's great eschatological teaching. Every believer from the time of Christ onward has been called to observe Christ's teaching in this manner.

A PLEA

At this point, I want to plead with you not to put down this book. Perhaps you hold to either preterism or pretribulationalism. I know of godly men and women who hold to both. If this describes you, it may be tempting to stop reading at this point because the book doesn't coincide with what you believe. But if the parable of the fig tree is for us to learn and apply, which I think the above arguments compellingly confirm, then understand that this command does not come from me. It comes from our common and glorious King.

I am confident that as you progress through this book, you will see further evidence that the Olivet Discourse holds essential teaching to the contemporary believer. We may or may not be the chosen group of believers to "see all these things." But we, like every generation since the resurrection of Christ, are called to learn, apply, and watch for Jesus' return *in the manner that He commanded.* In short, this parable applies to you, and you are called to learn its teaching. For one day "the rain will fall, the floods will come, and winds will blow." The church will encounter deception and persecution like it never has before. Therefore, it is of paramount importance that we build our house on the rock by hearing, learning, and applying the Lord's commands.

Let us now proceed to learn the initial "buds" we are to watch for regarding the figurative but ever-important fig tree.

End Notes 2

---

[1] Gary DeMar, *End Times Fiction* (Nashville: Thomas Nelson, 2001), 111.

[2] John MacArthur, *The Second Coming* (Downers Grove, IL: Crossway, 1999), 134.

[3] Ibid, 87–88.

[4] Both preterism and pretribulationalism will argue that the Olivet Discourse has a certain level of application to the church because they teach that there are principles and implications that may be applied. While this may be true, *direct applicability* is the issue. Therefore, both pretribulationalism and preterism do not teach that the Olivet Discourse directly applies to contemporary believers. Thus, in these paradigms, contemporary believers need not be concerned with looking for these signs.

[5] See G. Henry Waterman's work "The Sources of Paul's Teaching on the 2nd Coming of Christ in 1st and 2nd Thessalonians," *Journal of the Evangelical Theological Society*, 18 (1975), 105–13. This article explores and demonstrates the numerous links between the Thessalonian epistles and the Olivet Discourse. Also, New Testament scholar D. A. Carson notes that "the discourse itself is undoubtedly a source for the Thessalonian epistles" D.A. Carson "Matthew" in *The Expositor's Bible Commentary*, Ed. Frank E. Gaebelein, 12 Vols. (Grand Rapids: Zondervan, 1985), 8:489.

[6] Larry V. Crutchfield, "The Blessed Hope and the Tribulation in the Apostolic Fathers" in *When the Trumpet Sounds*, Thomas Ice, Timothy Demy, eds (Eugene: Harvest House, 1995), 103.

[7] See Charles Cooper, *God's Elect and the Great Tribulation* (Bellefonte, PA: Strong Tower Publishing, 2008), 75–77, for further evidence pertaining to this point.

[8] Samuel P. Tregelles, *The Hope of Christ's Second Coming* (Bellefonte, PA: Strong Tower Publishing, 2006), 75–76.

The Parable of the Fig Tree

3

THE BEGINNING BUDS

Understanding the Initial Signs of Christ's Return

As a father, I have become well acquainted with the birthing process. Of course, my wife would take great issue with the term "well acquainted." Observing the glorious, yet gut-wrenching process of bringing a new child into the world is a learning experience in more ways than one. The fact is, knowing the dynamics of this process helps us understand the parable of the fig tree. How? Because Jesus uses distinct yet related imagery at the inception of the Olivet Discourse. He likens the events of the end to the process of giving birth.

To mix the metaphors, the first "buds" that Jesus pronounces regarding the events relating to this parable are the beginning of birthpangs. "Birthpangs" is a figure of speech often used in end-times texts.

As is common in proper biblical interpretation, we must examine the context to see how the figure of speech is functioning in the text at hand. Here, Jesus has likened the first course of events to the *beginning of birthpangs*. To fully appreciate the analogy, we must step back and look at the whole of the Olivet Discourse. In doing so, we will be able to ascertain how the progress of end-times events relates to the birthing process and identify the "delivery" or end of the course of events. The way the events of the Olivet Discourse relate to the birthing process (which will be further established over the next several chapters) is this: As birthpangs increase in intensity as the delivery nears, so will the events that lead up to the end of the age. The events that Jesus outlines increase in intensity until we behold the glory of the deliverance of God's people and the coming of the Kingdom of God.

FIG TREE BUD #1: THE ARRIVAL OF FALSE CHRISTS

Our Lord's first warning in the Olivet Discourse should immediately sober us and draw us to close attention. The Discourse begins:

> And Jesus answered and said to them, "See to it that no one misleads you. For many will come in My name, saying, 'I am the Christ,' and will mislead many." (Matt. 24:5)

The first bud, or birthpang, is the arrival of false christs. We may be tempted to simply think of false christs as those who brazenly label themselves "the Christ." However, we must be careful to properly understand the point Jesus is making. Appreciating the underlying meaning of the term "christ" will help us understand the subtlety of false Christs and equip us to recognize those who seek to deceive both the world and the people of God.

The Greek word *christos* literally means "anointed one." Those who genuinely believe in the person and work of Jesus Christ confess there is one unique Anointed One, and that is the King Himself. He is the one who instructs us in the one true way to the Father and the authentic terms of the New Covenant. His message has been preserved in the scriptures in order to teach, guide, and protect us. Yet, there are those who arise, seeking to usurp His position as the Unique One. The methods and messages vary, but those who claim to speak for God and proclaim a way to God apart from Jesus' teaching are demonstrating themselves to be false "anointed ones." They proclaim a "peace" that is not granted by God's authority. These people place themselves in the position of an anointed lawgiver that only rightly applies to Jesus, *the* Christ. With this background, we can understand how false christs spread their seductive message. They claim a special anointing and proceed to mislead many through teaching the way to peace is to follow their teachings.

The end of the age will be marked by heightened deception. As we proceed to explore the Olivet Discourse, we will see that, as we approach the end of the age, this seduction intensifies. We are to see to it that no one deceives us, for there will be a great increase in those who claim to hold the position of the "anointed one" and will mislead many. Our calling is to cling to Christ and His words. We are to recognize that many will arise, seeking to take our eyes off the Chief Shepherd. By trusting Jesus alone, and by putting His commands into practice, we will faithfully navigate the seductive teachings of the false anointed ones as they arise.

FIG TREE BUD #2: WARS AND RUMORS OF WARS

The next budding event that will appear on the scene is explained by the Lord.

> "You will be hearing of wars and rumors of wars. See that you are not frightened, for those things must take place, but that is not yet the end." (Matt. 24:6)

From the Lord's instructions, we are to understand that the time prior to the end will consist of both wars and rumors of wars. "War" is to be understood as the "rising of nation against nation" in military battle. The added phrase "rumors of wars" refers to the threat or possibility of such action based on friction between kingdoms. Thus, national conflict is going to dominate the world climate in the days leading up to Christ's return. Jesus further highlights this in the first portion of the next verse—"nation will rise against nation and kingdom against kingdom" (Matt. 24:7).

While war and looming possibilities of international conflict will permeate the time prior to the end, our instructions are not to allow these things to distress us. We are commanded not to be frightened. The uprising of war and rumors of such should not scare us. Since these events have the potential to shake the Christian's soul, the Lord's words should both soothe us and sober us. They should soothe us in that Jesus is in complete control of the situation. These events are necessary precursors to the end. The phrase "these things must take place" indicates that they are sovereignly established and are setting the stage for the coming of the kingdom of Christ. While our Lord's sovereignty should soothe us, His command should sober us. We should strive to be at peace in Him. While the world around us may crumble, the heart fixed on the sufficient grace of Jesus Christ will be well prepared to not be frightened when such events begin to unfold.

FIG TREE BUD #3:
EARTHQUAKES AND FAMINES

As this section of the Olivet Discourse concludes, two further aspects of this time are revealed. While these are laid down as markers that will signal the nearing of Christ's coming, they also indicate further hardship that will announce the soon arrival of the King.

> "And in various places there will be famines and earthquakes. But all these things are merely the beginning of birth pangs." (Matt. 24:7–8)

39

There will be famines and earthquakes in "various places." This phrase points to the fact that such occurrences will not be concentrated in a particular area but will be widespread across the earth. When we combine these conditions with the widespread conflict and rising of false christs, it is apparent that unrest and upheaval in the religious, political, and environmental spheres define the "beginning of birthpangs."

At this point, it is important to pause and consider the phrase "beginning of birth pangs" and incorporate it into our worldview concerning the end of the age. Our Lord uses this phrase to clearly define the early period of time that leads to His coming. This indicates that Jesus is drawing upon the analogy of the birthing process to describe the distress that is evident prior to His return. Many may think: "All these things have been going on for two-thousand years. How am I to watch for these in light of this fact?" We do well to interact with this thought before proceeding.

UNDERSTANDING THE "LAST DAYS"

You may hear the phrase, "We are living in the last days" often repeated in the church. While there is truth in this statement, it may not be for the reason many think. In surveying the usage of the term "last days" in the New Testament, we find an interesting dynamic. Consider Peter's announcement at Pentecost, just after the Spirit was poured out:

"For these men are not drunk, as you
suppose, for it is only the third hour of the
day; but this is what was spoken of
through the prophet Joel: 'And it shall be
in the last days,' God says, 'that I will pour
forth of my Spirit on all mankind; and your
sons and your daughters shall prophesy,
and your young men shall see visions, and
your old men shall dream dreams; even on
my bondslaves, both men and women, I
will in those days pour forth of my Spirit
and they shall prophesy. (Acts 2:15–18,
emphasis added)

The apostle John uses similar language in his
first epistle.

Children, it is *the last hour*; and just as you
heard that antichrist is coming, even now
many antichrists have appeared; from this
we know that it is the last hour. (1 John
2:18, emphasis added)

These are just a sampling of the scriptures that
confirm that the "last days" were ushered in with the
first coming of Christ. According to the teaching of
Luke and Peter, the "last days" will consist of the Lord
pouring out His Spirit on all flesh and the continual
arising of counterfeit christs. The "last days," then,
will not *begin* with the second coming of Jesus, but
will be *consummated* by it.

When considering these things, there is an
underlying function to Jesus' words. Since these
events have, in some manner, been perpetually evident
during the last days, they should function in a manner

to keep us watchful and ready. False christs, war, earthquakes, and famines have been evident throughout the age of the church. In one sense, then, these birthpangs are already among us. Thus, these warnings function to keep us all watching and prepared for the next signs to appear on the scene of human history, regardless of the time period in which we live. In other words, in some manner, these events mark the whole age of the church.

In light of this, we must ask, is there *specific*, heightened application of these birthpangs to those who also witness the events leading to the end of the age? While in one sense these are already in our midst, there remains a future fulfillment. In order to understand this, we will establish the first of many parallels between the Olivet Discourse and the book of Revelation.

THE LAMB AND THE SCROLL

The book of Revelation is a gift from Christ to His church. The opening of the book makes this manifest:

> The Revelation of Jesus Christ, which God gave Him to show to His bond-servants, the things which must soon take place; and He sent and communicated it by His angel to His bond-servant John, who testified to the word of God and to the testimony of Jesus Christ, even to all that he saw. (Rev. 1:1–2)

Furthermore, the one who reads and heeds the instruction given in Revelation is rendered as blessed.

> Blessed is he who reads and those who
> hear the words of the prophecy, and heed
> the things which are written in it; for the
> time is near. (Rev. 1:3)

Far from being an elusive and fruitless endeavor, reading and heeding the book of Revelation is an essential activity for the bondservants of Jesus Christ. While John was on the Isle of Patmos, the resurrected Lord arrived and commanded him to write down "the revelation." After John received instructions to the seven churches in Asia Minor, he was taken to heaven before the glorious throne room of God. In the center of this magnificent scene was God the Father, holding in His hand a scroll lined with seven seals.

> I saw in the right hand of Him who sat on
> the throne a book written inside and on
> the back, sealed up with seven seals. (Rev.
> 5:1)

At this point, it is imperative that we understand the meaning of this scroll and its seals. This requires answers to two questions: What do the seals represent? What does the scroll contain? Answering these questions demands an understanding of the historical background of scrolls, their seals, and the flow of the book of Revelation.

The Scroll of Revelation

In the first century, scrolls were a primary means of communication. A scroll was a rolled up piece of parchment. In order to ensure that its contents were unaltered, the scroll was often fixed with a seal or seals. The only way to open the scroll and read its contents was to break the seals. Only after all the seals were broken could one open the scroll and read its contents. Often, one would write the inheritance due to an heir on a scroll and affix the scrolls with multiple seals. The seals represented prior conditions that needed to be met before the inheritance could be obtained. For instance, if one had an inheritance scroll secured by three seals, the heir had to meet three conditions before the inheritance could be obtained. For example, the first condition may have been that the heir had to pass the age of thirteen years. Once that was condition was met, the first seal could be broken. The second condition might have been that the heir had to marry. Once that condition was met, the second seal could be broken. The third condition might have been that the heir had to have a child. Once that condition was met, the third seal could be broken. Once all the conditions were met, the scroll could be opened, the contents read, and the inheritance obtained.[1]

44

Understanding this historical background, we can now ask: "What does this scroll contain?" A careful reading of Revelation indicates that this scroll is best understood as the title deed to the kingdom of God. Note that Jesus is the only one worthy to open the seals.

> And they sang a new song, saying, "Worthy are You to take the book and to break its seals; for You were slain, and purchased for God with Your blood men from every tribe and tongue and people and nation. You have made them to be a kingdom and priests to our God; and they will reign upon the earth." (Rev. 5:9–10)

Since Jesus is the only one worthy to break the seals, He is also the only one worthy to receive its contents, which is the kingdom of God coming in power upon the earth. Once all seven seals are opened, the wrath of God is poured out in the form of the seven trumpets (Revelation 8–11). As the contents of the scroll are completed with the final trumpet, we read:

> Then the seventh angel sounded; and there were loud voices in heaven, saying, "The kingdom of the world has become the kingdom of our Lord and of His Christ; and He will reign forever and ever." (Rev. 11:15)

Thus, we see that the seals are the prior conditions that need to be met before the scroll is opened and the wrath of God is poured out, culminating with "the kingdom of the world becoming the kingdom of our God and of His Christ."

One parallel we can already see with the Olivet Discourse is that the seals are prior conditions that need to take place before "the end" comes. Recall that the birthpangs were things that "must take place, but the end is not yet." Likewise, the seals are events that "must take place" before the end arrives. We are not to be frightened nor deceived, for the Lord is in control and guiding history towards its great and terrible consummation.

SEAL #1: THE ARRIVAL OF THE FALSE CHRIST

With the stage set and the background of the scroll explored, we can now proceed to behold the breaking of the first seal.

> Then I saw when the Lamb broke one of the seven seals, and I heard one of the four living creatures saying as with a voice of thunder, "Come." I looked, and behold, a white horse, and he who sat on it had a bow; and a crown was given to him, and he went out conquering and to conquer. (Rev. 6:1–2)

There are three clues to what this first horseman represents. The horseman rides on a white horse. He has a bow, and is given a crown. Jesus rides a white horse in Revelation 19, but in this context, Jesus is the one breaking the seals that release this horse and its rider. Thus, the rider cannot be Jesus. A bow (which represents conquest) and a crown (which represents authority) are granted to this rider. Given these elements that mimic the true Christ, along with the relationship with the other three horsemen, this rider is best viewed as representing the rising of the Antichrist and his kingdom.

Recall the first condition that Jesus announced in the Olivet Discourse. False christs will arise. Since the rider on the white horse is best viewed as the ultimate false christ (or "the beast," as Revelation refers to him), it is pertinent to note there is a parallelism that exists between the first birthpang Jesus described in the Olivet Discourse and the first seal broken in the book of Revelation. This parallelism will be further established as we see continued continuity between the Olivet Discourse and the seals. As we understand this seal and its implications, we should remember Christ's command regarding false christs: Do not be deceived by those proclaiming a false peace and safety. Only the Prince of Peace holds authentic peace between God and man brought about by His blood. Only those who flee to the Father through the Son will be safe from His coming wrath.

SEAL #2: WAR

Now remember the second condition Jesus announced as a precursor to the end of the age. Jesus declared that there would be "wars and rumors of wars. Nation will rise against nation and kingdom against kingdom" (Matt. 24:6). The parallels between the birthpangs and the seals continues:

> When He broke the second seal, I heard the second living creature saying, "Come." And another, a red horse, went out; and to him who sat on it, it was granted to take peace from the earth, and that men would slay one another; and a great sword was given to him. (Rev. 6:3–4)

A great sword was given to the second horseman, who rides a red horse, symbolizing bloodshed. A great sword was given to him that he might take peace from the earth and that men would slay one another. This describes the activity of war, corresponding with Jesus' declaration in the Olivet Discourse. As we proceed to the breaking of the third seal, the consistency continues.

SEAL #3: FAMINE

> When He broke the third seal, I heard the third living creature saying, "Come." I looked, and behold, a black horse; and he who sat on it had a pair of scales in his hand. And I heard something like a voice in the center of the four living creatures saying, "A quart of wheat for a denarius, and three quarts of barley for a denarius; and do not damage the oil and the wine." (Rev. 6:5–6)

The imagery of the third seal is uncommon to modern ears. The rider carries scales, which were used to weigh and dispense food. A denarius was a day's wage. Since both a quart of wheat and three quarts of barley each cost a denarius, this indicates vastly inflated food prices, a result of famine. Recall that the third birthpang Jesus noted in the Olivet Discourse was "famine and earthquakes" (Matt. 24:7). Thus, the parallels between the seals and the birthpangs continue with the third seal, with the indication that this period will be characterized by famine and food shortages.

With the compelling parallelism between the beginning of birthpangs and the first three seals, we can see that these events will carry specific application to the people who witness the unfolding of the end of the age. While these conditions have been evident throughout the church age, they will intensify and be markers of the time just prior to Christ's return.

THE PARABLE THUS FAR

Let's step back and incorporate these things into learning the parable of the fig tree. In this parable, we are called to take action on two fronts. First we are to recognize that these events are precursors to the end. They are birthpangs. They will intensify as we approach the "last days of the last days." Second, we are to hear and heed the Lord's exhortation to not be frightened by these things nor be deceived by those who would seek to mislead us. We must listen to the Lord that, though these things must come to pass, "the end is not yet." As we proceed, we will hear of further events that also must take place before the

Lord of Hosts arrives to rescue His people and repay the wicked.

Therefore, the first buds of the figurative fig tree that we are to look for, as confirmed by the first three seals of the book of Revelation, are false christs, wars and rumors of wars, and a time period characterized by famines and earthquakes.

As we proceed to the next section of the Lord's Olivet Discourse, we will see that there are further "buds" that we are to look for, there are further commands that need to be heeded, and the "labor" that will precede His coming and the gathering of His people will intensify. But in the midst of all these dark trials, the gospel of the kingdom of God and the hope of redemption will shine in all its glory.

End Notes 3

---

[1] There is a telling reversal of this tradition in the Lamb's opening of the scroll. The breaking of the seals produces the conditions that lead to the opening of the scroll. This demonstrates the sovereignty of the Lamb. All the conditions and events that follow from the breaking of the seals are under His control.

The Parable of the Fig Tree

4

TRIBULATION PAINS

Understanding the Final Campaign against God's Elect

Jesus described to us, in very clear detail, the signs that will signal the end of the age. These "beginning of birthpangs" are the rising of false christs, war, earthquakes and famine. With these signs now understood, they should be fixed in our sights. However, the Lord clearly established that the end is "not yet." There remains "hard labor" before the deliverance of God's people will occur.

Jesus uses birthing imagery in the farewell discourse in the gospel of John to describe what the disciples will go through in witnessing the death and resurrection of Christ.

> "Whenever a woman is in labor she has pain [*thlipsis*], because her hour has come; but when she gives birth to the child, she no longer remembers the anguish because of the joy that a child has been born into the world." (John 16:23)

53

The Greek word for "pain" in this text is *thlipsis*. This is the same word Jesus uses to describe what the faithful in Christ must endure immediately prior to His return. So after the beginning birthpangs are described in the Olivet Discourse, Jesus moves on to the hard labor that comes next.

> "Then they will deliver you to tribulation [*thlipsis*], and will kill you, and you will be hated by all nations because of My name." (Matt. 24:9)

The transition "then," and the context, indicate that the flow of the Discourse is describing what happens after the beginning of birthpangs. Jesus instructs His disciples—those who hold to the name of Jesus—that they will experience "tribulation." This term is used to describe affliction, trouble, or pain. The attitude of "all nations" toward believers in Christ at the time just prior to His return will be that of hatred. This hatred will be to the point that they will kill those who cling to His name.

What is terribly unfortunate is that the modern use of the word "tribulation" has departed from its biblical usage. The vast majority of the time I hear this term used in an end-times context, it is used refer to a general time of terror that God will pour out at the end of the age. In reality, the biblical usage of this term in the Olivet Discourse is the exact opposite. "Tribulation" here speaks of *the world* delivering believers to tribulation: persecution, hatred, and death. Therefore, in the Olivet Discourse, "tribulation" is not the pouring out of God's end-

54

times "day of the Lord" wrath, but rather the wicked action of the unbelieving world toward believers.

The fact is, believers were already experiencing harsh tribulation in the first century. As we survey the New Testament, we see that tribulation was a common theme for those who believed in the name of Jesus Christ. Note these examples:

> "These things I have spoken to you, so that in Me you may have peace. In the world you have tribulation [*thlipsis*], but take courage; I have overcome the world." (John 16:33)

> "Not only this, but we also exult in our tribulations, knowing that tribulation [*thlipsis*] brings about perseverance." (Rom. 5:3)

> You also became imitators of us and of the Lord, having received the word in much tribulation [*thlipsis*] with the joy of the Holy Spirit. (1 Thess. 1:6)

> But remember the former days, when, after being enlightened, you endured a great conflict of sufferings, partly by being made a public spectacle through reproaches and tribulations [*thlipsis*], and partly by becoming sharers with those who were so treated. (Heb. 10:32–33)

> After they had preached the gospel to that city and had made many disciples, they returned to Lystra and to Iconium and to Antioch, strengthening the souls of the

> disciples, encouraging them to continue in the faith, and saying, "Through many tribulations [*thlipsis*] we must enter the kingdom of God." (Acts 14:21–22)

What makes the tribulation described by Jesus in the Olivet Discourse unique from all other tribulations faced by the people of God throughout history? It is both its *scope* and *intensity*. Regarding this time of history, Jesus declares:

> "For then there will be a great tribulation [*megas thlipsis*], such as has not occurred since the beginning of the world until now, nor ever will." (Matt. 24:21)

Recalling the context, Jesus is describing a tribulation that believers will experience. This will be the last and greatest trial that the people of God will ever encounter. While the persecution of the church has been evident throughout her history, it has always been sporadic and localized. The "great tribulation" will be worldwide.

Let's return to the book of Revelation for further insight into the dynamics of this unparalleled time.

The Beast's War Against the Saints

Revelation chapters twelve through fourteen form an interlude in the midst of the progression of the trumpet and bowl judgments. Chapter twelve tells of the conflict of the ages between the Serpent and the seed of the woman, which comes to a culmination at the end of the age. In chapter thirteen, the campaign against God's people by the ultimate "man of lawlessness" or "Antichrist" is described by John, whom he labels "the beast":

> And he opened his mouth in blasphemies against God, to blaspheme His name and His tabernacle, that is, those who dwell in heaven. It was also given to him to make war with the saints and to overcome them, and authority over every tribe and people and tongue and nation was given to him. All who dwell on the earth will worship him, everyone whose name has not been written from the foundation of the world in the book of life of the Lamb who has been slain. (Rev. 13:6–8)

Note that "authority over every tribe, nation, and tongue" was given to this individual, and he is allowed "to make war with the saints and overcome them." These elements echo what we know regarding the time of tribulation about which Jesus instructs us in the Olivet Discourse. Jesus' disciples will be "hated by all the nations" and killed for their testimony of Jesus Christ. We are then given instructions from the inspired pen of John on what we are to do in this intense situation:

> If anyone has an ear, let him hear: If anyone is to be taken captive, to captivity he goes; if anyone is to be slain with the sword, with the sword must he be slain. Here is a call for the endurance and faith of the saints. (Rev. 13:9–10 ESV)

Since all the nations, under the leadership of the Antichrist, will be opposed to the true Christ and those who cling to Him, there will be great difficulty. The Christian is never promised a life free from difficulty and persecution. In fact, the opposite is promised. Paul writes, "Anyone who wishes to live godly in Christ Jesus will be persecuted" (2 Tim. 3:12). Some will be destined for captivity at this time; others will be killed. Therefore, the call to those who have "ears to hear" is to *endure*. Since God has promised to always be with His people, we are to trust His sovereign plan and power and be faithful, even to the point of death. In the book of Revelation, those who keep the faith are called "overcomers." Although God will permit this difficult time for a short time, not only will God keep His people, but He will vindicate them by sending His Son to wage war against those who persecute them.

THE GREAT APOSTASY

The grievous truth evident as we return to read Christ's teaching in the Olivet Discourse is that many will not endure in the truth. In light of all these difficulties, Jesus further explains the conditions that will mark this time:

> "At that time many will fall away and will betray one another and hate one another. Many false prophets will arise and will mislead many. Because lawlessness is increased, most people's love will grow cold." (Matt. 24:10–12)

In light of the tribulation that will be directed at God's people, many will fall away. This describes those who claim the name of Christ, but when difficulty comes and the love of the world beckons, they abandon their profession and turn to iniquity. The terms used here indicate that those who fall away are then aligned with the world in hatred towards Christ's people. They will join the "war against the saints" through betraying one another and hating one another. Jesus described these types of professors in the parable of the sower, recorded earlier in Matthew.

Note the parallels between Jesus' explanation of this parable and the events of the apostasy in the midst of this great tribulation:

> "Hear then the parable of the sower. When anyone hears the word of the kingdom and does not understand it, the evil one comes and snatches away what has been sown in his heart. This is the one on whom seed was sown beside the road. The one on whom seed was sown on the rocky places, this is the man who hears the word and immediately receives it with joy; yet he has no firm root in himself, but is only temporary, and *when affliction* [thlipsis] *or persecution arises because of the word, immediately he falls away.* And the one on whom seed was sown among the thorns, this is the man who hears the word, and *the worry of the world and the deceitfulness of wealth choke the word, and it becomes unfruitful.* And the one on whom seed was sown on the good soil, this is the man who

hears the word and understands it; who
indeed bears fruit and brings forth, some a
hundredfold, some sixty, and some thirty."
(Matt. 13:18–23, emphasis added)

This parable well applies to the circumstances
that define the period of tribulation that the church
will encounter prior to Christ's coming. The trial that
confronts those who claim the name of Christ will
serve as a great refining fire. This trial will separate
the wheat from the tares. It will reveal those whose
faith is genuine and those whose faith is superficial.
Those who have genuine faith, through the power of
the grace of God, will endure, despite all attempts to
overthrow their trust in the Almighty. Those who
have a superficial faith will fall away in the presence of
tribulation and the deceptive lusts of this world.

Immediately after giving the parable of the
sower, Jesus gives another parable that teaches on the
wheat and the tares. This parable again speaks
specifically to the conditions that define the time prior
to Christ's return.

Jesus presented another parable to them,
saying, "The kingdom of heaven may be
compared to a man who sowed good seed
in his field. But while his men were
sleeping, his enemy came and sowed tares
among the wheat, and went away. But
when the wheat sprouted and bore grain,
then the tares became evident also. The
slaves of the landowner came and said to
him, 'Sir, did you not sow good seed in
your field? How then does it have tares?'

And he said to them, 'An enemy has done
this!' The slaves said to him, 'Do you want
us, then, to go and gather them up?' But
he said, 'No; for while you are gathering
up the tares, you may uproot the wheat
with them. Allow both to grow together
until the harvest; and in the time of the
harvest I will say to the reapers, "First
gather up the tares and bind them in
bundles to burn them up; but gather the
wheat into my barn."'" (Matt. 13:24–30)

The agriculturalist will immediately understand
what Jesus is saying here. Both wheat and tares look
similar in their infant stages of growth. But once the
harvest time comes, their true nature is displayed.
Jesus proceeds to explain the meaning of the parable:

Then He left the crowds and went into
the house and His disciples came to Him
and said, "Explain to us the parable of the
tares of the field." And He said, "The one
who sows the good seed is the Son of Man,
and the field is the world; and as for the
good seed, these are the sons of the
kingdom; and the tares are the sons of the
evil one; and the enemy who sowed them
is the devil, and the harvest is the end of
the age; and the reapers are angels. So
just as the tares are gathered up and
burned with fire, so shall it be at the end
of the age. The Son of Man will send forth
His angels, and they will gather out of His
kingdom all stumbling blocks, and those
who commit lawlessness, and will throw

> them into the furnace of fire; in that place
> there will be weeping and gnashing of
> teeth. Then the righteous will shine forth
> as the sun in the kingdom of their Father.
> He who has ears, let him hear." (Matt.
> 13:36–43)

Given these truths laid out by our Master, our calling to endure is all the more highlighted. Those who endure will be saved. The ones who retain their testimony, even in the midst of the greatest trial and persecution, will "shine forth as the sun in the kingdom." In contrast, those who have the appearance of being believers but in fact are not will be revealed for what they truly are, then judged by the King of creation.

As we proceed to further explore the Olivet Discourse and the book of Revelation, we will see the dynamics taught in this parable further explained. Therefore, returning to the flow of the Olivet Discourse, the next exclamation by the Lord resounds true: "But the one who endures to the end, he will be saved" (Matt. 24:13).

ENDURING TO THE END

The Lord's requirements for those in this time are clear. Nothing short of "enduring to the end" is acceptable. If standing for the gospel costs believers their lives, they have endured. If they are allowed to remain to the coming of the Lord and are faithful, they have endured. However, if one ceases to persevere and aligns with the world, he has fallen away.

Endurance is a quality that is stressed throughout the Bible. From Genesis to Revelation, those who endure hardship and temptation and abide in the Almighty are the ones who are blessed. From Abraham, Job, and Joseph to Peter, Paul, and the ultimate example, Jesus, those who endure are "conquerors." The call to endure is all the more highlighted in a time when endurance will be most difficult. Deception and persecution will press in on all sides. The need for endurance is necessary and noted by our sovereign Master.

THE SEALS CONTINUED

In the last chapter, we left off with the flow of the seals in the book of Revelation at seal three, which told of great famine. Since a pattern of parallelism was seen between the seals and birthpangs, we should expect these parallels to continue. Recalling that the Olivet Discourse promises there to be great trial and tribulation for the people of God, let's continue to read what the fourth seal teaches us about the time leading to the end.

SEAL #4: AUTHORITY TO KILL

When the Lamb broke the fourth seal, I heard the voice of the fourth living creature saying, "Come." I looked, and behold, an ashen horse; and he who sat on it had the name Death; and Hades was following with him Authority was given to

> them over a fourth of the earth, to kill
> with sword and with famine and with
> pestilence and by the wild beasts of the
> earth. (Rev. 6:7–8)

Here we see that this fourth rider is given authority over a fourth of the earth. The question is: Is this fourth of the earth *geographic* or *demographic?* In other words, does it refer to land or population? Since the authority given is "to kill," the best reading is that this refers to a fourth of the population of humankind. This text does not say that a fourth of the earth will actually be killed. Rather, it says that authority (or permission) will be given by God to kill through the means of sword, famine, pestilence, and the beasts of the earth.[1] Since "death and Hades" are the threat, the redeemed can stand firm, knowing that earlier our Lord announced, "I have the keys to death and Hades" (Rev. 1:18).

In light of the parallels to the Olivet Discourse, I believe the best reading of this fourth seal is the authority given to the Antichrist to make war with the people of God. "Sword, famine, and pestilence" are the means "the beasts" use to make war. This "authority" echoes what we read in both Daniel and Revelation regarding the activity of the Antichrist.

> "He will speak out against the Most High
> and wear down the saints of the Highest
> One, and he will intend to make
> alterations in times and in law; and they

64

will be given into his hand for a time,
times, and half a time." (Dan. 7:25)

Further exposition on this point will be given in
the next chapter. As we proceed to the fifth seal, we
read of the results of the fourth seal, which further
lends credence to the above interpretation.

SEAL #5: THE CRY OF THE MARTYRS

> When the Lamb broke the fifth seal, I saw
> underneath the altar the souls of those who
> had been slain because of the word of God,
> and because of the testimony which they
> had maintained; and they cried out with a
> loud voice, saying, "How long, O Lord, holy
> and true, will You refrain from judging and
> avenging our blood on those who dwell on
> the earth?" And there was given to each of
> them a white robe; and they were told that
> they should rest for a little while longer,
> until the number of their fellow servants
> and their brethren who were to be killed
> even as they had been, would be completed
> also. (Rev. 6:9–11)

Taking the fourth and fifth seals together, we
can see parallels between these seals and the events
Jesus reveals in the Olivet Discourse. There will be
great tribulation, where believers are hated and killed
for their testimony of Jesus. God's wrath upon the
world has not begun at this time, as the martyrs are
asking "how long" until the sovereign Lord deals out
retribution. The divine response is that once the last

martyr gives his life, the Lord will begin His systematic fiery wrath upon the wicked world. Why were these souls under the altar of God killed? Because they held firm to the testimony of the gospel. As we return to the Olivet Discourse, we see that the gospel of the kingdom is carried to the nations in this intense time of spiritual war.

> "This gospel of the kingdom shall be preached in the whole world as a testimony to all the nations, and then the end will come." (Matt. 24:14)

While "all the nations" are hatefully persecuting God's people, the good news of the kingdom will be preached as a *testimony*. The gospel of the kingdom will have an intensified function just prior to the end of the age. The word "gospel" means "good news." A careful reading of the New Testament reveals that the good news was ushered in with the first coming of Jesus Christ. His redemptive work secured eternal salvation for all who would believe in Him. The kingdom of God is already present in that the King has come and is now gathering His constituency from every tribe, nation, and tongue. But it is "not yet" in that God has not judged the world and set up His kingdom on earth.

The good news of the kingdom, in the context of the Olivet Discourse, is that the risen Lord is returning to deal with all injustice and repay all wickedness. The calling will go out to the nations to repent and believe in Jesus to escape the imminent wrath that is about to unfold. This is a testimony, or last warning, to the unbelieving world. Many will be killed for arising at this time and announcing, "Repent, for the kingdom of God is at hand." Once this is accomplished, the end will come. Human history will come to its culmination when the rightful King returns to cleanse the earth through fire and set up His kingdom.

While there is a great spiritual battle at this time, the way to victory for the faithful of God will not be to pick up physical swords. The way to victory will be to cling to our spiritual sword, which is the Word of God. Through his king, the Antichrist, Satan will make war with the saints. The way to overcome is to cling to the testimony of the gospel, no matter the consequences. The way to victory is laid out:

> And they overcame him because of the blood of the Lamb and because of the word of their testimony, and they did not love their life even when faced with death. (Rev. 12:11)

Although the great enemy of our souls will wage war with us, the blood of Jesus Christ secures us. His grace causes us to cling to the testimony of the gospel. Even though many who believe may be considered as "sheep for the slaughter" (Rom. 8:36), we who believe "overwhelming conquer through Him who loved us" (Rom. 8:37).

ANOTHER PLEA

I once again am compelled to plea with you not to put down this book. I am fully aware that many of these things are not popular, nor is imagining the possibility of having to endure such a time a pleasant thought. However, the remnant can concur with the early church that "through many tribulations must we enter the kingdom of God." I will echo what I wrote in the first chapter: We need to allow the scriptures to train our beliefs and form our worldviews. When the truth confronts us through the Word of God, we need to bow to its teaching, regardless of how emotionally difficult it may be.

In all these things, let's remember Jesus' analogy of childbirth noted at the beginning of this chapter. When the hour of childbirth comes, there is pain and sorrow. But once the baby is born, the sorrow is forgotten. In the same manner, though the time of trial will be difficult, the salvation of Christ's people will bring joy greater than can be imagined. We will be discussing these exciting truths soon. Not only will believers behold the glory of their redemption, but also the terrifying judgment of those who persecute and kill God's precious children.

THE PARABLE THUS FAR

Through understanding the events and conditions that Jesus describes in the Olivet Discourse, we learn the parable of the fig tree. Thus, by hearing the

Lord's instruction, we can see that following the beginning birthpangs (false christs, war, famines, and earthquakes), there will be "great tribulation" for the people who believe in Jesus Christ. There will be persecution and hatred for God's elect. In the wake of this persecution and difficulty, many will fall away. There will be a great apostasy. In the midst of this dark, unparalleled time of trouble for Christ's church, the glorious gospel will be proclaimed and *then* the end will come.

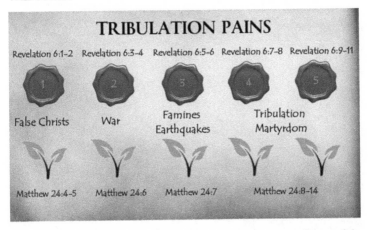

Jesus' teaching and instruction regarding this time is not complete. Our King will now proceed to teach on the specifics of this time, both describing the sign that begins this great tribulation and the sign that will terminate it.

End Notes 4

[1] "Wild beasts" is a deficient translation in this text as the Greek word used here is always translated "beasts" throughout the book of Revelation and either refers to the Antichrist or the false prophet. Inserting the word "wild" here when it is not in the text obscures this link.

5

THE ABOMINATION OF
DESOLATION

Understanding the Sign that Reveals the Antichrist
And Heralds the Beginning of the Great Tribulation

I n the Olivet Discourse, there are two signs that
nearly jump off the page. While all of the events
that Jesus outlines are signs that herald His
return, there are two that stand out from all the
others. One is the sign that will reveal the identity of
the Antichrist and the beginning of the great
tribulation. The other is the sign that will lead to the
revelation of Jesus Christ to rescue His elect and pour
out His wrath.

We need to patiently wait to explore the sign
that triggers the return of Christ (chapter seven), but
next in the progression of Jesus' Olivet Discourse is
the sign that reveals the Antichrist and the resulting
final campaign against God's people. Recall that we left

the flow of the discourse with Jesus telling of the great tribulation, the need to endure, the testimony of the gospel of the kingdom, and *then* the end will come. With the general flow of events established, Jesus turns with an important transition, beginning the next portion with "therefore" (24:15). The astute reader will recognize that Jesus is now going to give specific details and instructions regarding the time He just explained, the time that immediately precedes His return. It is hard to overstate the significance of the next portion of the discourse, as it provides a powerful scriptural link that gives great insight into Jesus' instruction. Jesus continues:

> "Therefore when you see the abomination of desolation which was spoken of through Daniel the prophet, standing in the holy place (let the reader understand)" (Matt. 24:15)

Jesus explicitly links His teaching to the prophet Daniel. Therefore, in order to understand Jesus' allusion, we need to turn back in our Bibles to the book of Daniel. There we will find a wealth of insight and teaching that will flesh out the Lord's end-times teaching in the Olivet Discourse

"LET THE READER UNDERSTAND"

In verse 15, the reader is exhorted to "understand." In order to understand the nature and significance of the abomination of desolation, we need to understand the teaching of the book of Daniel. In the wake of the exile of Israel and the Babylonian captivity, the Lord raised up a prophet, Daniel, in an alien land. There was a prophesied seventy-year exile that Daniel knew was about to come to an end (Dan. 9:2). In light of this, Daniel fervently prayed for His people and the city of Jerusalem. In response to this godly prayer, the Lord sent His answer via an angelic messenger. It is in this context that we learn much about the time Jesus is prophesying in the Olivet Discourse.

> He gave me instruction and talked with me and said, "O Daniel, I have now come forth to give you insight with understanding. At the beginning of your supplications the command was issued, and I have come to tell you, for you are highly esteemed; so give heed to the message and gain understanding of the vision." (Dan. 9:22–23)

The messenger Gabriel proceeds to give Daniel a new prophecy regarding the future of Israel and the city of Jerusalem. While the seventy-year captivity was about to expire, the Lord's purposes for Israel were going to be further revealed.

THE SEVENTY SEVENS

> "Seventy 'sevens' are decreed for your people and your holy city to finish transgression, to put an end to sin, to atone for wickedness, to bring in everlasting righteousness, to seal up vision and prophecy and to anoint the most holy. (Dan. 9:24 NIV)

It is within the explanation of this decree that we are given insight into God's redemptive plan for Israel and, by extension, the entire world.

Several interpretive notes are in order here. First we need to understand the meaning of the prophecy. Since Daniel was praying for His people and His holy city, the object of the prophecy is both the ethnic people of Israel and the historic city of Jerusalem. When these seventy sevens are complete, all of these promises and prophecies will be accomplished (bringing in everlasting righteousness, making an end to sin, anointing the most holy, and so on). At the time of Daniel's prayer, both Israel and Jerusalem were under discipline for idolatry and unfaithfulness to God. In the angel's answer, Daniel receives a contrasting response. Restoration and redemption are coming, but there will be further delay. There are seventy sevens decreed for Israel and Jerusalem.

The Hebrew word for "seven" here is *shabua*. It simply means a unit of seven. The historical understanding is virtually unanimous that these are seventy sevens of *years*. The Hebrew year consists of 360 days. Thus, 490 years (of 360 days) are decreed for the people of Israel and the holy city until the plan of redemption is fulfilled. After the objects (Israel and Jerusalem) and purpose (fulfillment of the plan of redemption) are proclaimed, several specifics are set forth in Daniel 9:25–27.

THE FIRST 69 SEVENS

"Know and understand this: From the issuing of the decree to restore and rebuild Jerusalem until the Anointed One, the ruler, comes, there will be seven 'sevens,' and sixty-two 'sevens.' It will be rebuilt with streets and a trench, but in times of trouble." (Dan. 9:25 NIV)

Gallons of ink have been devoted to trying to ascertain the beginning and end of the first sixty-nine weeks. There is a division, 7 sevens and 62 sevens that comprise the first 69 sevens. Several plausible explanations have been given to how these first 69 sevens were fulfilled. However, given the various drawbacks that plague each interpretation, this author does not have clarity regarding how *specifically* the first sixty-nine weeks were fulfilled. This does not mean there are not compelling historical suggestions on when these were fulfilled. In fact, the opposite is the case.

There are several well thought out scenarios that may correctly identify the beginning and end of the first 69 sevens (483 years) of the prophecy. One of the most popular is Sir Robert Anderson's articulation in the nineteenth century work *The Coming Prince*. This interpretation sees the beginning of the 70 sevens with Artaxerxes' decree in Nehemiah 2 to rebuild Jerusalem. Anderson (and others who have refined his model) calculated that 483 years (69 sevens) from the date given in this text would bring us to the royal entry when Jesus, the Anointed One, rode into

Jerusalem. Others, such as Charles Cooper[1], have pointed out some problems with this interpretation and suggested that the fulfillment of the first 69 sevens fits better with other historical events, all which conclude with events in the first century.

While this author awaits further clarity on the *exact* fulfillment of the first 69 "sevens," three issues are evident regarding this prophecy: 1) the first sixty-nine sevens have passed, beginning with the rebuilding of Jerusalem in the fifth century B.C. and reaching their end sometime in the first century; 2) there is a "gap" or delay between the 69th seven and the 70th seven; and 3) the 70th "seven," or final seven-year period, is situated on the horizon of human history.[2]

Let's consider the teaching on this final seven in this prophecy, as it is what Jesus called us to understand in the Olivet Discourse.

THE FINAL SEVEN: A COVENANT AND AN ABOMINATION

> The people of the ruler who will come will destroy the city and the sanctuary. The end will come like a flood: War will continue until the end, and desolations have been decreed. He will confirm a covenant with many for one "seven." In the middle of the "seven" he will put an end to sacrifice and offering. And on a

wing of the temple he will set up an abomination that causes desolation, until the end that is decreed is poured out on him. (Dan. 9:25–27 NIV)

Daniel writes of the last seven-year period that will complete the 70 sevens prophecy. This last seven is defined by two events: a covenant and an abomination. The prince of the people who will come is a human ruler who will confirm a seven-year covenant with "the many," which is a term often used for the people of Israel. However, in the middle of this seven, or three-and-a-half years after confirming the covenant, this ruler will set up an "abomination that causes desolation." Pay attention here. This is what our Lord called us to look for. Remember our Master exhorted: "When you see the abomination of desolation, spoken of through the prophet Daniel (let the reader understand)" (Matt. 24:15).

What is the "abomination of desolation?"

THE ABOMINATION OF DESOLATION: WHAT *WAS* AND *WILL BE*

When the original Jewish audience heard the term "abomination of desolation," they would have immediately recognized Jesus' reference. A foreshadow of the Antichrist had already lived and acted by the time Jesus spoke these words on the Mount of Olives. The seeds of prophecy are in history. In using the term "abomination of

77

desolation," Jesus draws upon historical, fulfilled prophecy to proclaim what is to come.

Around the year of 167 B.C., a Greek ruler who named himself Antiochus Epiphanes IV (which translated means "Antiochus, manifest god") invaded the city of Jerusalem and desecrated the temple. His exploits were recorded in the book of 2 Maccabees.

> When these happenings were reported to the king, he thought that Judea was in revolt. Raging like a wild animal, he set out from Egypt and took Jerusalem by storm. He ordered his soldiers to cut down without mercy those whom they met and to slay those who took refuge in their houses. There was a massacre of young and old, a killing of women and children, a slaughter of virgins and infants. In the space of three days, eighty thousand were lost, forty thousand meeting a violent death, and the same number being sold into slavery. Not satisfied with this, the king dared to enter the holiest temple in the world. (2 Macc. 5:11–15)

Furthermore, 2 Maccabees 6 records:

> Not long after this the king sent an Athenian senator to force the Jews to abandon the customs of their ancestors and live no longer by the laws of God; also to profane the temple in Jerusalem and dedicate it to Olympian Zeus, and that on Mount Gerizim to Zeus the Hospitable, as the inhabitants of the place requested.

This intensified the evil in an intolerable and utterly disgusting way. (2 Macc. 6:1–3)

The first-century Jewish historian Josephus chronicled this event in this manner:

And when the king built an idol altar upon God's Altar, he slew swine upon it, and so offered a sacrifice neither according to the law, nor the Jewish religious worship in that country. He also compelled them to forsake the worship which they paid their own God, and to adore those whom he took to be gods; and made them build temples, and raise idol altars, in every city and village, and offer swine upon them every day.[3]

Daniel foretells of this man and his work in chapter eleven:

Forces from him will arise, desecrate the sanctuary fortress, and do away with the regular sacrifice. And they will set up the abomination of desolation. (Dan. 11:31)

Therefore, "the abomination of desolation" was understood as the act of Antiochus ransacking Jerusalem, stopping the customs of the Jews, and setting up a Greek god in the sanctuary. This abomination was a sign of the desolation that resulted: death and bloodshed by one who opposed God and His people.

This occurred around 167 B.C. Jesus' exhortation took place around A.D. 30. The implications of His instructions are sobering: *the abomination of desolation has yet to occur.*

"THEN THERE WILL BE GREAT TRIBULATION"

After reading Daniel and understanding how the "abomination of desolation" was understood as in the first century, we can now continue with Jesus' words in the Olivet Discourse with further clarity.

> Therefore when you see the *abomination of desolation* which was spoken of through Daniel the prophet, standing in the holy place (let the reader understand), then those who are in Judea must flee to the mountains. Whoever is on the housetop must not go down to get the things out that are in his house. Whoever is in the field must not turn back to get his cloak. But woe to those who are pregnant and to those who are nursing babies in those days! But pray that your flight will not be in the winter, or on a Sabbath. For *then* there will be a great tribulation, such as has not occurred since the beginning of the world until now, nor ever will. (Matt. 24:15–21 emphasis added)

The abomination of desolation spoken of in Daniel 9:27 is yet to occur. The parallels between the events of Antiochus' siege and what is described in Matthew 24:15–21 are evident. The epicenter is the city of Jerusalem. A desecration of a temple is involved. Anyone in Judea (in the modern day, the greater area of Jerusalem) is called to flee. For those in Judea, there is no time to be concerned with physical possessions. The siege will be intended to destroy. When these events are seen, we are to know that "then there will be a great tribulation, such as has not occurred since the beginning of the world until now, nor ever will" (v. 21).

In this discourse, the Lord has already described many of the details that mark this time: hatred, betrayal, apostasy, and tribulation (vv. Matthew 24:9–10). Here this time is described as "great tribulation." Keeping in mind what we learned in the last chapter, that tribulation in this context is the ungodly persecution of God's people, this period of time Jesus describes has no comparison. It has not occurred yet, nor will it ever occur again. This will be the ultimate persecution against the people of God for all time. It is "great" (Greek *megas*) because of both its scope and intensity. Persecution of God's people (both the church and Israel) has always been sporadic and localized. The campaign against God's elect at the end of the age will be universal across all nations. The sign that the "great tribulation" is upon us is the *abomination of desolation*. When Jerusalem is sieged and the temple in Jerusalem is treated in a comparable way to what occurred in 167 B.C., we are to recognize the "great tribulation" is upon us.

THE WAR OF THE SERPENT

In the book of Revelation, John writes a parallel account to the time Jesus describes. In Revelation 12, we read a synopsis of the war of the ages. The serpent (Satan) persecutes the woman (Israel). Apparently, there will be those who flee Jerusalem to safety, though they are fiercely pursued by the enemy.

> Then the woman fled into the wilderness where she had a place prepared by God, so that there she would be nourished for one thousand two hundred and sixty days. (Rev. 12:6)

Notice the "woman" (a remnant of Israel) flees to the wilderness for 1260 days. This is three-and-a-half Jewish years, where God protects this group until the end of the 70th seven. But where there is protection from God, we also read of persecution from the Serpent.

> And when the dragon saw that he was thrown down to the earth, he persecuted the woman who gave birth to the male child. But the two wings of the great eagle were given to the woman, so that she could fly into the wilderness to her place, where she was nourished for a time and times and half a time, from the presence of the Serpent. And the Serpent poured water like a river out of his mouth after the woman, so that he might cause her to be swept away with the flood. But the

> earth helped the woman, and the earth
> opened its mouth and drank up the river
> which the dragon poured out of his mouth.
> So the dragon was enraged with the
> woman, and went off to make war with
> the rest of her children, who keep the
> commandments of God and hold to the
> testimony of Jesus. (Rev. 12:13–17)

Satan will be thrown down to earth, and his immediate aim of destroying Israel will be thwarted. He will then "make war" with those who keep the commandments of God and hold to the testimony of Jesus. These are God's elect—the church, the "called out" ones. This describes how this tribulation will begin in Jerusalem and Judea and then spread throughout the whole world. This war will be waged through the "beast," John's term in Revelation for the Antichrist. As we read into chapter thirteen of Revelation, we are given understanding of this unparalleled time of persecution through the person of the beast.

> There was given to him a mouth speaking
> arrogant words and blasphemies, and
> authority to act for forty-two months was
> given to him. And he opened his mouth in
> blasphemies against God, to blaspheme
> His name and His tabernacle, that is,
> those who dwell in heaven. It was also
> given to him to make war with the saints
> and to overcome them, and authority over
> every tribe and people and tongue and
> nation was given to him. (Rev. 13:5–7)

83

Forty-two months (three-and-one-half years) was given to the beast "to act." This is the last half of the 70th seven. The "activity" given to the Antichrist was to make war with the saints. This will be a time of "great tribulation" because of its intensity and because this man who declares war against God's elect has authority over "every tribe and people and tongue and nation." But our God is sovereign. He reigns over every minute, every action, and every soul in the midst of this time of trouble. As the fifth seal is opened in Revelation, those who lose their lives in this war cry out to God for justice. John writes:

> When the Lamb broke the fifth seal, I saw underneath the altar the souls of those who had been slain because of the word of God, and because of the testimony which they had maintained; and they cried out with a loud voice, saying, "How long, O Lord, holy and true, will You refrain from judging and avenging our blood on those who dwell on the earth?" And there was given to each of them a white robe; and they were told that they should rest for a little while longer, until the number of their fellow servants and their brethren who were to be killed even as they had been, would be completed also. (Rev. 6:9–11)

When the last martyr gives his life, the time will be fulfilled. The Lord of Hosts will arise and call upon his army of angels to bring fire and wrath to the world that persecuted His people. But there is a delay. Those in heaven and those on earth must *wait*.

WHY THE DELAY?

When reflecting on the 70 sevens prophecy of Daniel 9, there is a clear delay between the 69th and 70th seven. As I write these words, nearly two-thousand years have passed. Why the wait? In the wisdom of God, He planned to build the constituency of His kingdom through the preaching of the gospel. The gospel of Jesus Christ goes forth to every tribe, nation, and tongue. Those who repent and believe the gospel are constituents of the kingdom of God. The delay is for the Spirit to go forth, gathering members of the kingdom of Christ through the power of the gospel. This plan was a "mystery" before Christ came, but it is now revealed through His apostles and prophets. Note Paul's teaching in Ephesians 3:4–6:

> By referring to this, when you read you can understand my insight into the mystery of Christ, which in other generations was not made known to the sons of men, as it has now been revealed to His holy apostles and prophets in the Spirit; to be specific, that the Gentiles are fellow heirs and fellow members of the body, and fellow partakers of the promise in Christ Jesus through the gospel.

Gentiles are fellow partakers of the promise in Christ Jesus through the gospel. The 70th seven will be the time when God consummates His purposes for both Israel and the church. We will behold how this plan is beautifully consummated as we further explore the scriptures in the coming chapters.

PARABLE OF THE FIG TREE

As we have learned in this chapter, Jesus' allusion to Daniel gives us great insight into the dynamics of this time He is predicting. Daniel received revelation of a timetable of 70 sevens for the people of Israel and the city of Jerusalem. As of this writing, there has been nearly two-thousand years between the 69th and 70th seven. The last seven-year period, which is God's final consummating work with Israel and the church, is divided in two parts. It begins with a confirmed covenant, and three-and-one-half years into this covenant, Jerusalem will be sieged and the abomination of desolation will be set up in the temple. This is a sign for us to understand. It heralds the arrival of the great tribulation, but it also heralds the imminent return of Jesus Christ. When we see these things, we are to "recognize He is near, right at the door."

To summarize, now we can view the "buds of the fig tree" within the timeframe established in Daniel:

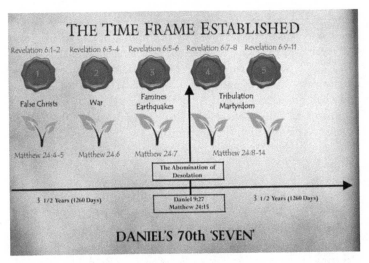

THE TIME FRAME ESTABLISHED

Because this time will be one of great trial, there will be great temptation to escape. But we must realize that the only way we will escape this time unscathed is through faithfully observing the commands of Christ. False prophets and false christs will flood the land. For those who may find themselves in this unparalleled epoch, we need to carefully hear our King's instructions as we await His return in glory. This is our next endeavor.

End Notes 5

[1] Charles Cooper, *God's Elect and the Tribulation* (Bellefonte, PA: Strong Tower Publishing, 2009).

[2] Examining the three primary end-times New Testament texts (the Olivet Discourse, the Thessalonians epistles, the book of Revelation) demand such a view. The Olivet Discourse speaks of a future fulfillment of the abomination of desolation. Both the Olivet Discourse and the Thessalonian epistles establish that this

event will be shortly followed by the return of Christ in glory. Furthermore, the book of Revelation references the last half of Daniel's 70th seven in three different ways: forty two months (Rev. 13:5); twelve hundred and sixty days (Rev. 11:3); and time, times, and a half time (Rev. 12:14). All of these points help us understand the historical fulfillment of the 70 sevens prophecy: the first 69 sevens were finished in the first century and there is an unrevealed delay until the 70th seven transpires and these prophecies are fulfilled.

[3] Flavius Josephus, *The Antiquities of the Jews* as published in the larger work *The Works of Josephus, Complete and Unabridged* New Updated Edition (Translated by William Whiston, A.M.) (Peabody Massachusetts: Hendrickson Publishers, 1987 [Fifth Printing: Jan.1991]: *The Antiquities of the Jews* Book 12, Chapter 5, verse 253 (p. 324).

6

LIKE LIGHTNING

Hearing Christ's Instructions for This Unparalleled Time

False prophets and false christs have been around for as long as their counterparts. Whenever the Lord acts, the enemy counterattacks. Jesus has warned us from the inception of the Olivet Discourse that we must not be deceived. How are we called to avoid deception? By hearing the words of Christ and putting them into practice. This principle is of the utmost importance when it comes to Jesus' exhortations to His people who encounter the time of great tribulation.

In the Olivet Discourse, Jesus describes the sign that triggers the great tribulation, the abomination of desolation. This tribulation will start in Jerusalem and reverberate through the entire world. As Jesus warned, "They will deliver you to tribulation, and will kill you, and you will be hated by all nations because of My name" (Matt. 24:9). In order to accomplish this, the Serpent will send out his false

89

christs and false prophets to deceive and destroy. To combat this, the true Christ gives His people important instructions:

> "Then if anyone says to you, 'Behold, here is the Christ,' or 'There He is,' do not believe him. For false christs and false prophets will arise and will show great signs and wonders, so as to mislead, if possible, even the elect. Behold, I have told you in advance." (Matt. 24:23–25)

Jesus' words are intended to awaken us. He has told us in advance. We are without excuse. The intense peril of this time is evident in this exhortation. This tribulation will be so severe, and the level of deception so great, that these deceivers could mislead the elect (if that were possible). Since this warning is so serious, we first need to understand the message of these deceivers. Then we need to understand their aim. Finally, we need to understand their means of deception.

The message of the false prophets and christs in this time will be to deceive about the timing and place of Christ's coming. Our Lord declares that false prophets will arise and declare, "Here is the Christ" or "There He is." The aim of this is to draw people away from the words of the true Christ. Those who do not heed Christ's admonition will either be deceived and aligned with the Antichrist or drawn away and killed. Remember, the aim of the Serpent is to deceive and destroy. In order to accomplish this, the false prophets and false christs will be equipped with supernatural signs and wonders.

A close reading of the scriptures that speak of the time just prior to Christ's return reveals that "lying signs and wonders" will abound. In 2 Thessalonians, Paul warns strongly against deception and tells of the powers that will be displayed by these agents of evil.

> Then that lawless one will be revealed whom the Lord will slay with the breath of His mouth and bring to an end by the appearance of His coming; that is, the one whose coming is in accord with the activity of Satan, with all power and signs and false wonders, and with all the deception of wickedness for those who perish, because they did not receive the love of the truth so as to be saved. For this reason God will send upon them a deluding influence so that they will believe what is false, in order that they all may be judged who did not believe the truth, but took pleasure in wickedness. (2 Thess. 2:8–12)

The Antichrist and his minions will be equipped with power, signs, and false wonders. All those who do not believe the truth of the gospel of Jesus Christ will be judged. We see evidence in this text that God specifically allows this deluding influence in order to separate the wheat from the tares. Those who believe in the truth will be faithful and delivered. Those who do not will be judged because they did not receive the love of the truth. These are hard truths that do not echo often from today's pulpits. Yet, these words are Spirit-breathed and should sober the believing heart to be on the alert.

Deception abounds in today's world. Subtle, sinister forces are continually seeking to draw hearts and minds away from the truth of Jesus Christ. What we see today is merely a sneak preview of the massive deception that will unfold just prior to Christ's return. Not only does the Olivet Discourse and Paul's second epistle to the Thessalonians warn of this deception, but so does the book of Revelation. In chapter thirteen, John describes the activity of the beast and the second beast, who is often dubbed "the false prophet."

> Then I saw another beast coming up out of the earth; and he had two horns like a lamb and he spoke as a dragon. He exercises all the authority of the first beast in his presence, and he makes the earth and those who dwell in it to worship the first beast, whose fatal wound was healed. He performs great signs, so that he even makes fire come down out of heaven to the earth in the presence of men. And he deceives those who dwell on the earth because of the signs which it was given him to perform in the presence of the beast. (Rev. 13:11–14)

All three major end-times texts of the New
Testament (the Olivet Discourse, the Thessalonian
epistles, and Revelation) concur that lying signs and
wonders will mark the end of days. These signs and
wonders will deceive, and the whole world will be
engaged in blatant, unrestrained idolatry. Those who
refuse to comply with this campaign of deception will
be persecuted, some unto death. Jesus noted that these
signs and wonders will be so convincing that they
could deceive even the elect. But He added a qualifier:
"if that were possible." The function of this statement
is to awaken the reader to the intensity of the
deception. The good news is that God's elect are
preserved by *His power*.

In his second letter to the Thessalonians, Paul
addresses this issue and provides comfort to those
destined to endure this terrible time. Right after Paul
warns his readers about the coming man of
lawlessness, his deceptive signs and wonders, and the
judgment that awaits those who follow him, Paul
turns his attention to God's elect.

> But we should always give thanks to God
> for you, brethren beloved by the Lord,
> because God has chosen you from the
> beginning for salvation through
> sanctification by the Spirit and faith in the
> truth. It was for this He called you
> through our gospel, that you may gain the
> glory of our Lord Jesus Christ. So then,
> brethren, stand firm and hold to the
> traditions which you were taught,

> whether by word of mouth or by letter
> from us. (2 Thess. 2:13–15)

The signs and wonders will be severely seductive, but they will not be able to snatch believers from the hand of their Savior. Because this is true, we are all the more called to "stand firm and hold to the traditions" we are taught in the scriptures. Even though we are secure, it is still imperative that we hear and heed our Lord's instructions for the end.

Jesus continues His teaching regarding this time of trouble.

> "So if they say to you, 'Behold, He is in the wilderness,' do not go out, or, 'Behold, He is in the inner rooms,' do not believe them. For just as the lightning comes from the east and flashes even to the west, so will the coming [*parousia*] of the Son of Man be." (Matt. 24:25–26)

The instructions of our Lord are clear. We should never be deceived about whether or not He has returned. If someone says He is in the "wilderness," meaning the outer areas where many false christs peddled their teachings in the first century, we are not to believe it. If someone says the Lord has returned and is in the "inner rooms," meaning in earthly hiding and about to be brought forth, we are not to believe it. Our Lord then tells His church how we will recognize His return. At His first coming, Jesus arrived in humble circumstances. He was laid in an animal trough. This signified the nature of His first visitation—to be the Suffering Servant, the perfect Lamb of God who takes away the sin of the world, drawing the meek and humble to Himself. At His second coming, it will not be to bear the sins of the world, but to deliver those who are anxiously awaiting Him, then to deal out retribution to those who do not obey His gospel. This coming will be "like lightning."

The metaphor of lightning is to be understood in contrast to "out in wilderness" or "in the inner rooms." Lightning that flashes is visible from the east and from the west. Everyone sees it. Such manifestation is visible to all. In the same way, when Jesus returns, there will be no question as to whether or not the Messiah has come. Every eye will see Him (Rev. 1:3). We will not be left wondering whether Jesus has returned. When He comes back, it will be in power and glory. All will see and all will know that the King of Kings has returned, and His return is in power and wrath.

This is further highlighted with the cryptic statement: "Wherever the corpse is, there the vultures will gather" (Matt. 24:28). Given the context that "all will see" His return, the phrase "corpse and vultures" further emphasizes this imagery. Whenever there is a rotting corpse, you know vultures will be there. Circling vultures are a clear sign of death. Even so, when the Son of Man is revealed, every eye will see the Lamb, and those who have opposed Him will be judged. His coming will mean salvation for those who

95

believe, but for those who do not, it will be sheer terror because the Judge has returned for the day of reckoning.

HIDING HIS INSTRUCTIONS IN OUR HEARTS

We do well to recognize the seriousness of Jesus' words: "Behold, I have told you everything in advance" (v. 20). Though this time that our Lord outlines is marked with trial and sorrows, our Shepherd cares for us. He has given us these instructions for our preparation and good. We need to hide these words in our hearts: When Jesus returns, everyone will know it. If someone tries to tell you different, do not believe them. We need to take seriously the danger of deception. If someone attempts to undermine the words of Christ and teach you principles that are opposed to His instructions, do not believe them. Though we always must be on the alert, we also are called to rest in the loving arms of our Savior. No matter how strong the pull of deception or how intense the pain of persecution, no one can pluck God's elect from the grip of His grace.

THE PARABLE THUS FAR

Our Lord has further outlined the events and conditions that herald His return. The beginning of the end will be heralded by a very specific set of signs: the rise of false christs, wars, famines, and earthquakes. Jesus labeled these "the beginning of birthpangs." Jesus then describes a time of great distress and persecution for God's people. There will be betrayal, apostasy, and martyrdom. The event that signals the beginning of this unparalleled time is the abomination of desolation. This describes the siege of Judea and the abominable desecration of the temple in Jerusalem. The persecution will begin in Judea and spread through the whole world. This will be a time of great deception during which false prophets and false christs abound. We are not to be deceived by their words or signs and wonders, as Jesus promised that His return will be unmistakable. It will be like lightning, visible to all, and every eye will see Him.

In describing the intensity of persecution upon the people of God during this time, Jesus declares, "Unless those days had been cut short, no life would have been saved; but for the sake of the elect those days will be cut short" (Matt. 24:22). After God's people have endured much hardship, they now arrive at the event they are all anxiously awaiting—the return of Jesus Christ. Jesus has just declared that His coming will be like lightning. The Father has something special planned for the return of His Son. Just when it looks as if the world has won—just when Satan's king is reigning, apostasy is rampant, Jerusalem is sacked, the church is scattered, and many have been killed—the Lord of heaven and earth will arise and say "No more!" But before the sky is ignited with the glory of God the Son, the sign of His coming occurs. The skies will be prepared for the Son.

7

PREPARING THE SKIES FOR THE SON

*Understanding the Sign that Heralds
The Return of Jesus Christ*

I t is an event that has been eagerly anticipated for thousands of years. After He accomplished the mission of His first visitation, the risen Lord and His disciples went back to the Mount of Olives, the very place He gave His end-times discourse. In the wake of giving His final instructions, our King ascended into heaven.

> And after He had said these things, He was lifted up while they were looking on, and a cloud received Him out of their sight. And as they were gazing intently into the sky while He was going, behold, two men in white clothing stood beside them. They also said, "Men of Galilee, why do you stand looking into the sky?

> This Jesus, who has been taken up from
> you into heaven, will come in just the
> same way as you have watched Him go
> into heaven." (Acts 1:9–11)

Jesus' descent from heaven at His visible second coming will not disappoint in its glory and impact. While His ascension into the clouds was viewed by a select few, His return will be seen by all. It will be cause for the righteous to rejoice and the wicked to wail. We have come to the point in the Olivet Discourse where the Lord is going to intervene and judge all the nations that oppose His people and His purposes. As we will see, however, the Olivet Discourse is not the first time we see this event described in scripture. The promised "Day of the Lord" had been anticipated throughout the prophetic scripture, even long before the first coming of Christ. In Matthew 24:29–30, we read:

> "But immediately after the tribulation of
> those days *the sun will be darkened, and the
> moon will not give its light, and the stars will
> fall from the sky*, and the powers of the
> heavens will be shaken. And then the sign
> of the Son of Man will appear in the sky,
> and then all the tribes of the earth will
> mourn, and they will see the Son of Man
> coming on the clouds of the sky with
> power and great glory."

Jesus proclaims that the great sign that will signal His immediate return is the cosmic light sources going dark. The lights that rule either the day or the night will not give their light. The entire world

100

will be plunged into total darkness. The world will be going about its business, eating, drinking, and being given in marriage. Suddenly, that which is taken for granted—the shining of the sun and the light of the moon—will be taken away. There will be two responses to this sign. The wicked will wail and hide in the rocks, while the redeemed will stand and rejoice, for their Warrior and Deliverer is arriving.

THE SIXTH SEAL

We have progressed through the breaking of the seals in Revelation chapter six. As we have seen, there are clear parallels to the events Jesus outlines in the Olivet Discourse. Seals one through three parallel the beginning of birthpangs. Seals four and five parallel the events of the great tribulation. Now we have come to the sixth seal. As we see, the parallels continue:

> I looked when He broke the sixth seal, and there was a great earthquake; and the sun became black as sackcloth made of hair, and the whole moon became like blood; and the stars of the sky fell to the earth, as a fig tree casts its unripe figs when shaken by a great wind. The sky was split apart like a scroll when it is rolled up, and every mountain and island were moved out of their places. Then the kings of the earth and the great men and the commanders and the rich and the strong and every slave and free man hid themselves in the caves and among the rocks of the mountains; and they said to

101

> the mountains and to the rocks, "Fall on
> us and hide us from the presence of Him
> who sits on the throne, and from the
> wrath of the Lamb; for the great day of
> their wrath has come, and who is able to
> stand?" (Rev. 6:12–17)

The parallels are striking. When the heavenly
bodies go dark, there will be a great earthquake and
the people of the earth will mourn, recognizing that
the great day of God's wrath has come. The prophet
Joel likewise spoke of this sign and proclaimed that
this sign precedes the great day of God's wrath.

> "I will display wonders in the sky and on
> the earth, blood, fire and columns of
> smoke. The sun will be turned into
> darkness and the moon into blood before
> the great and awesome day of the Lord
> comes." (Joel 2:30–31)

The day of the Lord will be sudden and
terrifying for those who oppose God.[1] He will throw
those who are in spiritual darkness into physical
darkness, and they will not escape. Paul speaks of the
coming wrath of the Lamb in 1 Thessalonians 5. The
apostle exhorts:

> Now as to the times and the epochs,
> brethren, you have no need of anything to
> be written to you. For you yourselves
> know full well that the day of the Lord
> will come just like a thief in the night.
> While they are saying, "Peace and safety!"
> then destruction will come upon them
> suddenly like labor pains upon a woman

with child, and they will not escape. But
you, brethren, are not in darkness, that the
day would overtake you like a thief. (1
Thess. 5:1–3)

A thief comes in the night. He comes
unexpectedly. When Jesus returns, the world will not
be expecting it. They will have bought into the system
of Babylon. They will be united under one ruler (the
Antichrist). From the midpoint of the 70th seven until
this sign, the Antichrist will give the world what it
wants—peace, safety, and dark spiritual power. Those
who unite under him will be saying, "Peace and
safety!" But one day (the time we do not know, for we
don't know the time or epochs), Jesus will arrive
suddenly and the world will not escape His wrath.

Believers, however, are not in spiritual darkness.
When the lights of the universe are turned down, we
who trust in Jesus and do not fall prey to the enemy's
deception will respond quite differently than the
world. Jesus' end-times discourse in Luke declares
what our response should be when we see these
things come to pass.

> "There will be signs in sun and moon and
> stars, and on the earth dismay among
> nations, in perplexity at the roaring of the
> sea and the waves, men fainting from fear
> and the expectation of the things which
> are coming upon the world; for the
> powers of the heavens will be shaken.
> Then they will see the Son of Man
> coming in a cloud with power and great
> glory. But when these things begin to

take place, straighten up and lift up your
heads, because your redemption is
drawing near." (Luke 21:25–28)

Men will be fainting from fear when such
mainstays as the sun, moon, and stars are darkened.
The response of the redeemed will be different. The
event for which we have longed has drawn near.
While the world dives into the rocks and hides from
the power and wrath of God, Jesus tells His people to
straighten up and lift up their heads. Those who have
endured the persecution of the Antichrist and resisted
the worldwide deception are called to arise. The
imagery of "straightening up" and "lifting up your
heads" calls to mind the demonstration of hope and
vindication. The contrast is striking. Those who have
not believed the truth will faint from fear. They will
dive into the rocks, realizing God's wrath is imminent.
They are about to enter eternal punishment away
from the presence of God. Those who trust in Jesus
Christ, who have been persecuted and in the midst of
a "tribulation never to be equaled," will lift up their
heads, realizing their *redemption* is imminent. The
redeemed are about to enter into the bliss and joy of
their Master.

THE COMING OF THE SON OF MAN

The scene is set. The wicked are wailing and frantic
regarding what is coming upon them. The redeemed
are lifting up their heads and rejoicing because their
King is coming to rescue them. With the world

plunged into darkness and the earth shaking, the sky is ignited with the power and glory of Jesus Christ.

> And then the sign of the Son of Man will appear in the sky, and then all the tribes of the earth will mourn, and they will see the Son of Man coming on the clouds of the sky with power and great glory. (Matt. 24:30)

This is the time of vindication. The Lord's ambassadors and prophets will have gone out and proclaimed to the world: Repent and believe in Jesus Christ, for He is returning. The Lord's bondservants will be met with contempt, scoffing, and malice. But in the midst of utter darkness, the glory of the Lord will ignite the sky. Every eye will see Him, and all the tribes of the earth will mourn.

"COMING IN THE CLOUDS"

Jesus' coming on the clouds of the sky should be viewed as a literal prophecy, but we also must be sure to recognize what this signifies. In the book of Daniel, the outline of human history is prophesied. Throughout the book, the "kingdoms of this world" are foretold and their ultimate demise assured. Why? Because an unshakable kingdom will be established and have a King that rules this eternal realm.

> "I kept looking in the night visions, and behold, with the clouds of heaven. One like a Son of Man was coming, and He came up to the Ancient of Days. And was presented before Him. And to Him was

105

given dominion, glory and a kingdom, that all the peoples, nations and men of every language might serve Him. His dominion is an everlasting dominion which will not pass away; and His kingdom is one, which will not be destroyed. (Dan. 7:13–14)

When every eye sees Jesus coming in the clouds, it is a public manifestation of the King of Kings. This is the one who rules the kingdom of God forever. This coming in the clouds will publicly and powerfully declare that the kingdom of this world is going to pass away and the kingdom of Christ will be set up forever.

WHEN WILL THESE THINGS BE?

A question that we naturally ask, and the one asked by the disciples, was *when*? When will the Lord return? Recall the question that prompted the discourse:

As He was sitting on the Mount of Olives, the disciples came to Him privately, saying, "Tell us, when will these things happen, and what will be the sign of Your coming, and of the end of the age?" (Matt. 24:3)

When we understand the whole of the Olivet Discourse and the command to learn the parable of the fig tree, we can understand how Jesus answered their question. In fact, His answer is summarized in Matthew 24:32–36:

"Now learn the parable from the fig tree: when its branch has already become tender and puts forth its leaves, you know that summer is near; so, you too, when you see all these things, recognize that He is near, right at the door. Truly I say to you, this generation will not pass away until all these things take place. Heaven and earth will pass away, but My words will not pass away. But of that day and hour no one knows, not even the angels of heaven, nor the Son, but the Father alone."

The Lord's answer to the disciples' question—*when?*—is summarized in this text. No one but the Father knows the day, the hour, of the Lord's return. However, the season has been revealed. The disciples asked for *the* sign. Jesus' answer gave them several signs. When these conditions are seen, we are to recognize He is near. When the sun, moon, and stars do not give their light, we straighten up and lift our heads because He is "at the door."

Therefore, taking Jesus' words in context, no man knows the day or hour of His return. This has not been revealed by the Father. However, we are commanded to recognize the *season* of His return.

IMMEDIATELY AFTER THE "TRIBULATION OF THOSE DAYS"

Jesus declares that the sign in the sun moon and stars and His coming will occur immediately after the tribulation of those days. Some have taken this to mean that this will occur immediately after the 1260 days prophesied in Daniel, at the very end of the last half of the 70th seven. However, this is not compelling for two reasons. First, Jesus stated that "no man knows" the day or hour of His return. Since no one knows this, we cannot calculate that He will return immediately after 1260 days of the last half of Daniel's 70th seven. Furthermore, earlier in the discourse, the Lord declares that "unless those days had been cut short, no life would have been saved; but for the sake of the elect those days will be cut short" (Matt. 24:22). The Greek word for "cut short" here is *koloboo*, which means "to amputate." For the sake of His elect, the Lord is going to amputate the days of persecution and tribulation. They will not run their full duration. The Lord will come at an unknown day and hour *after* the birthpangs, *after* the abomination of desolation is revealed, and *after* the tribulation of God's people has run its divinely allowed course, but *before* He pours out His indignation.

What then is meant by "after the tribulation of those days" if it is not speaking of a definite time period (such as the 1260 days)? Recall the Lord's answer to the cry of the martyrs after the opening of the fifth seal. They cried, "How long, O Lord?" until He would judge the earth. The divine answer was this: "They should rest for a little while longer, until the number of their fellow servants and their brethren who were to be killed even as they had been, would be completed also" (Rev. 6:11).

When will the church get relief and the world retribution? Second Thessalonians 1:6–8 answers this question in relation to this church.

> For after all it is only just for God to repay with affliction those who afflict you, and to give relief to you who are afflicted and to us as well, when the Lord Jesus will be revealed from heaven with His mighty angels in flaming fire, dealing out retribution to those who do not obey the gospel of our Lord Jesus.

Therefore, immediately after the last martyr gives his life for the testimony of Jesus Christ, the Lord will arise and go forth to wage war with those who oppose Him. Thus, it will take place immediately after the activity of "tribulation" and immediately before His wrath.

THE PARABLE OF THE FIG TREE

With all of these things established, the parable of the fig tree can now be properly understood. By God's grace, may we fix all these events, conditions, and commands delivered by our Lord in our spiritual sights. We must do this so that if these things come to pass on our watch, we will be able to recognize the signs of the times and remain faithful in the midst of the greatest trial the people of God will ever encounter.

The beginning buds of the figurative "fig tree" are the arising of false christs, wars, rumors of wars, famines, and earthquakes. If we see these things, we are to not be frightened because the end is "not yet."

Conditions will become very difficult for the people of God. Those who hold to the name of Jesus Christ and His teachings will be hated by all the nations. The sign of the abomination of desolation will herald the onset of events during which a man will arise and lead a siege of Jerusalem, beginning a persecution that reaches to the ends of the earth. False christs and false prophets will arise to deceive. The redeemed must realize that when Jesus returns, everyone will know it. They must not listen to those who would say otherwise.

The Lord will shut down all the light sources in the cosmos and arrive in power and glory. The world will wail and the redeemed will rejoice.

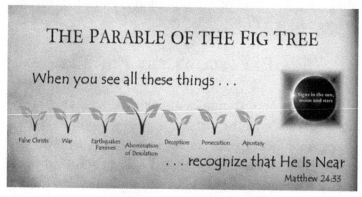

With all of these things understood, a very pressing question remains. When does the rapture occur? In the sequence of end-times events, when is the great gathering of God's elect? This important issue is what we will now explore.

End Notes 7

---

[1] The day of the Lord is a complex theological concept. Old Testament scholar Walter Kaiser helps give the background to the usage of this term in the New Testament: "[T]his day always had an impending nature to it. Though it found partial fulfillment in such events as Joel's locust plagues, the destruction of Jerusalem and the threat of national invasions, its final climactic fulfillment always remained in Christ's future return." Walter Kaiser, *Hard Sayings of the Old Testament* (Downers Grove: Intervarsity Press, 1988), 225.

The Parable of the Fig Tree

8

THE GREAT GATHERING

OF GOD'S ELECT

Understanding the Timing of the Rapture

What is the blessed hope of every believer? It is the glorious appearing of our Lord Jesus Christ. The term "blessed hope" comes from Titus 2:3: "looking for the blessed hope and the appearing of the glory of our great God and Savior, Christ Jesus."

The text describing this wonderful event in its detail is 1 Thessalonians 4:13–17. This is called by many the "classic rapture passage." The church in Thessalonica was grieving because brothers and sisters in Christ had died before the Lord had returned. They wondered, "What of those who have died?" In order to comfort their anxious souls, the apostle Paul taught of our blessed hope.

> For if we believe that Jesus died and rose
> again, even so God will bring with Him

113

those who have fallen asleep in Jesus. For
this we say to you by the word of the
Lord, that we who are alive and remain
until the coming of the Lord, will not
precede those who have fallen asleep. For
the Lord Himself will descend from
heaven with a shout, with the voice of the
archangel and with the trumpet of God,
and the dead in Christ will rise first. Then
we who are alive and remain will be
caught up together with them in the
clouds to meet the Lord in the air, and so
we shall always be with the Lord.
Therefore comfort one another with these
words. (1 Thess. 4:14–18)

With such exciting and comforting promises
before us, we may echo the question of the disciples,
"When?" As if in answer, Paul states: "Now as to the
times and the epochs, brethren, you have no need of
anything to be written to you" (1 Thess. 5:1).[1] The
times and epochs are fixed by the Father, but we are
not in darkness that this day should overtake us like a
thief (5:4). Still we ask, "When in the sequence of end-
times events does this occur?"

In the Olivet Discourse, Jesus describes His
coming. It will be in power and glory. It will also be to
gather His people from one end of sky to the other.

"And then the sign of the Son of Man will
appear in the sky, and then all the tribes of
the earth will mourn, and they will see the
Son of Man coming on the clouds of the
sky with power and great glory. And He

will send forth His angels with a great trumpet and they will gather together His elect from the four winds, from one end of the sky to the other. (Matt. 24:30–31)

In the "classic" rapture passage in 1 Thessalonians 4:14–18, there are numerous parallels and allusions to Jesus' teaching to the Olivet Discourse.

MATTHEW 24:30-31	1 THESSALONIANS 4:16-17
•The Lord Issues a Command (V. 30)	•The Lord Issues a Command (V. 16)
•A Trumpet Sounds (V. 31)	•A Trumpet Sounds (V. 16)
•Angelic Involvement (V. 31)	•Angelic Involvement (V. 16)
•Jesus Comes in the Clouds (V. 30)	•We Meet the Lord in the Clouds (V. 17)
•The Gathering of the Elect Takes Place in the Sky (V. 31)	•Those in Christ are Caught up Together in the Air (V. 17)

The parallels strongly suggest that Matthew 24:30–31 and 1 Thessalonians 4:16–17 are describing the same event. The confusion regarding the issue of resurrection in Thessalonica may have resulted from the fact that Jesus' description of His second coming in the Olivet Discourse does not explicitly state a

115

resurrection. Paul's writing clarifies this aspect of this event. Since the timing of the rapture is a very important and contested area of eschatology, it is time to engage two prominent viewpoints of the timing of the gathering of God's elect.

THE PRETRIBULATIONAL POSITION

Over the last one hundred and fifty years, the pretribulational position has become immensely popular in the Christian community. A plethora of books, novels, movies, and bumper stickers sing of this view of the timing of the rapture. The pretribulational position holds a distinction between the rapture and second coming. In this paradigm, the rapture described in 1 Thessalonians occurs prior to Daniel's 70th seven. The second coming occurs approximately seven years later. While the rapture debate has raged for decades and the discussions can be very detailed and complex, I am going to focus on two scriptures that I believe make a pretribulational rapture untenable.

THE "PAROUSIA"

The term used to describe the second coming of Christ throughout much of the New Testament is the Greek word *parousia*. This word is a noun that describes an event. In the Olivet Discourse, it is used frequently. One instance that is very significant to the question of the timing of the rapture occurs in Matthew 24:

"Then if anyone says to you, 'Behold, here is the Christ,' or 'There He is,' do not believe him. For false christs and false prophets will arise and will show great signs and wonders, so as to mislead, if possible, even the elect. Behold, I have told you in advance. So if they say to you, 'Behold, He is in the wilderness,' do not go out, or, 'Behold, He is in the inner rooms,' do not believe them. For just as the lightning comes from the east and flashes even to the west, so will the coming [*parousia*] of the Son of Man be. (Matt. 24:23–27)

Let us recall what we learned about this passage. These exhortations are given in the midst of the great tribulation. These are instructions for those in the wake of the abomination of desolation that occurs at the midpoint of Daniel's 70th seven. Jesus begins His instruction with "then," meaning "at that time."[2] Jesus does not want His followers to be deceived about the nature and timing of His coming (*parousia*). It will not be secret or quiet. If anyone declares the "Lord has returned," we are not to listen. No one will be guessing or wondering whether the Lord has returned. His coming (*parousia*) will be like lightning for all to see.

How then does this point relate to the 1 Thessalonians passage and the timing of the rapture? If we look at Paul's terminology and compare it with Jesus' teaching, we are compelled to see that the gathering of which Paul speaks in 1 Thessalonians must take place after the abomination of desolation. In describing the rapture in verses 15–17, he explicitly places this at the *parousia*.

> For this we say to you by the word of the Lord, that we who are alive and remain until the coming [*parousia*] of the Lord, will not precede those who have fallen asleep. For the Lord Himself will descend from heaven with a shout, with the voice of the archangel and with the trumpet of God, and the dead in Christ will rise first. Then we who are alive and remain will be caught up together with them in the clouds to meet the Lord in the air, and so we shall always be with the Lord. (1 Thess. 4:15–17)

According to the apostle Paul, the rapture occurs at the *parousia* of Jesus Christ. But Jesus warns those who are in the midst of the last half of Daniel's seventieth seven to not be deceived regarding people who say the *parousia* has already taken place (for example, He is in the "inner rooms" or "He is out in the wilderness"). The *parousia* will be visible, powerful, and will take place "immediately after the tribulation of those days." Therefore, the rapture described in 1 Thessalonians 4:14–18 *cannot* be pretribulational.

As if this were not enough evidence, we now turn to 2 Thessalonians. Paul wrote this book in response to further confusion regarding eschatological events that plagued the church at Thessalonica. A false report had come into the church asserting that they were already in the Day of the Lord. If true, this would have meant that they had missed the gathering to Christ. In 1 Thessalonians 4 and 5, Paul clearly tied the gathering of the elect to the Day of the Lord. These terms are again expressed in 2 Thessalonians 2:1–2. Note the expository links below:

The Connection of Terms in the Thessalonians Epistles

1 Thessalonians 4:15-5:2

For this we say to you by the word of the Lord, that we who are alive and remain until the coming (parousia) of the Lord, will not precede those who have fallen asleep. For the Lord Himself will descend from heaven with a shout, with the voice of the archangel and with the trumpet of God, and the dead in Christ will rise first. Then we who are alive and remain will be caught up together with them in the clouds to meet the Lord in the air, and so we shall always be with the Lord. Therefore comfort one another with these words. Now as to the times and the epochs, brethren, you have no need of anything to be written to you. For you yourselves know full well that the day of the Lord will come just like a thief in the night.

2 Thessalonians 2:1-2

Now we request you, brethren, with regard to the coming (parousia) of our Lord Jesus Christ and our gathering together to Him, that you not be quickly shaken from your composure or be disturbed either by a spirit or a message or a letter as if from us, to the effect that the day of the Lord has come.

Since the Day of the Lord is God's wrath, and being "we are not destined for wrath" (1 Thess. 5:10), the rapture must occur before God's wrath is poured out. Paul boldly steps in and gives this instruction:

> Now we request you, brethren, with
> regard to the coming [*parousia*] of our Lord
> Jesus Christ and our gathering together to
> Him, that you not be quickly shaken from
> your composure or be disturbed either by a
> spirit or a message or a letter as if from us,
> to the effect that the day of the Lord has
> come. *Let no one in any way deceive you, for it
> will not come unless the apostasy comes first,
> and the man of lawlessness is revealed, the son
> of destruction, who opposes and exalts himself
> above every so-called god or object of worship,
> so that he takes his seat in the temple of God,
> displaying himself as being God.* Do you not
> remember that while I was still with you,
> I was telling you these things? (2 Thess.
> 2:1–3, emphasis added)

If we have become well acquainted with the
parable of the fig tree, Paul's teaching here makes
perfect sense. The coming of the Lord and our being
gathered to Him, which occurs at the inception of the
Day of the Lord, cannot come unless the apostasy
occurs and the man of lawlessness is revealed—the
one who "takes His seat in the temple of God,
displaying himself as being God." Paul gives two
signs; two of the "buds," so to speak, of the figurative
fig tree. These things must occur before the Day of
the Lord. They must occur before "the coming of our
Lord and our being gathered to Him."

First, the apostasy. Jesus said there would be
great apostasy just prior to His return. In Matthew

24, verse 10–12: "At that time many will fall away and will betray one another and hate one another. Many false prophets will arise and will mislead many. Because lawlessness is increased, most people's love will grow cold."

Second, the man of lawlessness must be revealed. The means of his "revelation" is that he takes his seat in the temple of God. Jesus told us that when we see the abomination of desolation (Matt. 24:15, Jerusalem will be sieged and there will be great tribulation. The foreshadow of Antichrist, Antiochus, sacked Jerusalem, did abominable acts in the temple, and named himself "Epiphanes," which means "god manifest." The Antichrist will follow in his footsteps, seiging Jerusalem, taking his seat in the temple, and displaying himself as God.

There is no confusion between Paul and Jesus, only consistency and clarity. Take heed. Our Lord has told us in advance.

THE PRETERIST POSITION

As cited earlier, preterism is an increasingly popular paradigm of eschatology. It comes in two primary varieties: partial and full. *Partial preterism* holds that the whole of the Olivet Discourse was fulfilled in the destruction of Jerusalem in A.D. 70.[3] Adherents to this view still believe in a future coming of Christ and that 1 Thessalonians 4:14–18 speaks of the future resurrection. *Full preterism* believes that the Olivet

Discourse was fulfilled in A.D. 70, but so was the rapture and resurrection proclaimed in 1 Thessalonians 4. These adherents believe the resurrection is already passed and are rightly viewed by both partial preterists and futurists as outside the realm of the "faith delivered once and for all."[4]

The partial preterist position is one that is held by many Christians and scholars. One of the reasons is their understanding of "this generation" in Matthew 24:34. This *misunderstanding* will be addressed in chapter eleven. The partial preterist paradigm falls apart when one considers the inconsistency regarding the relationship between the Thessalonians epistles and the Olivet Discourse. Partial preterists insist that we understand the whole of the Olivet Discourse as being fulfilled in A.D. 70. However, if we look at the teaching of Paul in both of his Thessalonian epistles, we see a multitude of allusions and references to the Olivet Discourse that demand a yet-future fulfillment.

Note the allusions and references documented in the following chart:

Allusions to the Olivet Discourse In the Thessalonian Epistles

2 Thessalonians 2:8: Great signs and wonders accompany
The coming of the man of lawlessness
-Allusion to Matthew 24:15,24-

2 Thessalonians 1:7: Relief from persecution and
Tribulation occurs when Jesus is revealed
-Allusion to Matthew 24:29-

1 Thessalonians 4:15-16: Christ descends at the parousia
-Allusion to Matthew 24:30-36-

1 Thessalonians 4:16: Angels accompany Jesus at His parousia
-Allusion to Matthew 24:31-

1 Thessalonians 5:2-3: Sudden destruction comes upon the world
-Allusion to Matthew 24:37-39-

Since Paul drew upon the Olivet Discourse to teach about the second coming (*parousia*) of Christ, and since the resurrection of believers occurs at this time (1 Thess. 4:16–17), the position of the partial preterist becomes untenable. Most preterists see the "gathering" of Matthew 24:31 as describing the gospel going out to the nations. But Paul uses the terminology of the Olivet Discourse to describe the gathering of God's elect in the air. Those who are caught up and raised will experience total transformation. Note Paul's teaching in 1 Corinthians 15:

> For since by a man came death, by a man
> also came the resurrection of the dead. For
> as in Adam all die, so also in Christ all will

be made alive. But each in his own order:
Christ the first fruits, after that those who
are Christ's at His coming [*parousia*]" (1
Cor. 15:21–23)

Behold, I tell you a mystery; we will not
all sleep, but we will all be changed, in a
moment, in the twinkling of an eye, at the
last trumpet; for the trumpet will sound,
and the dead will be raised imperishable,
and we will be changed. (1 Cor. 15:51–52)

The resurrection occurs at the *parousia* of
Christ, and this point is the same problem that plagues
the pretribulationalist. Jesus speaks of His *parousia*, or
"coming," in the Olivet Discourse. It will be
unmistakable. If Paul declares that, at the time of the
parousia, the dead and Christ will rise and those who
are alive will be caught up, then the Olivet Discourse
cannot be primarily teaching on the destruction of
Jerusalem in A.D. 70. The only alternatives are the
heresy of full preterism or the consistency of
futurism. Given its inconsistency, the preterist
paradigm falls apart. In context, believing that both
the Olivet Discourse and the teaching of the
Thessalonian epistles are describing events that are yet
future is the only viable, biblical alternative.

THE GREAT MULTITUDE

We have already seen compelling parallels between the
Olivet Discourse, the Thessalonian epistles, and the
seals of Revelation. Now we are given the scene we

have all been waiting for. In the book of Revelation, we left off at the sixth seal. The heavenly bodies did not give their light, the whole earth shook, and the wicked were diving into the rocks. The righteous were told to "straighten up" and "lift up their heads," for their redemption was drawing near. We then heard in the Olivet Discourse that Jesus sent His angels to gather His elect. Paul confirmed this in 1 Thessalonians. How does John's writing in Revelation also confirm these things?

In Revelation 7, we are between the sixth and seventh seals. The seventh seal is the last seal of the scroll. When the seal is broken and the scroll is opened, the wrath of God is going to be poured out upon the world in a systematic manner. Remember the parable of the wheat and tares. The Lord was going to bind the tares to be burned and gather His wheat into His barn (Matt. 13:24–30). Revelation 7 describes this time:

> After this I saw four angels standing at the four corners of the earth, holding back the four winds of the earth, so that no wind would blow on the earth or on the sea or on any tree. And I saw another angel ascending from the rising of the sun, having the seal of the living God; and he cried out with a loud voice to the four angels to whom it was granted to harm the earth and the sea, saying, "Do not harm the earth or the sea or the trees until we

have sealed the bond-servants of our God
on their foreheads." (Rev. 7:1–3)

The drama is thick. There is calm with no wind.
God's wrath is about to be unleashed. But before this
occurs, God ensures that His bondservants will not
be touched by His wrath. Revelation 7:4–8 tells of the
sealing of 144,000 Israelites. I believe these are the
firstfruits of saved Israel. Though they are still on
earth, they are sealed and thereby protected from the
wrath of God. But what of everyone else? The dead
have just been raised and those still alive are caught up
with all the saints to be with the Lord forever. We see
this glorious scene in heaven.

> After these things I looked, and behold, a
> great multitude which no one could count,
> from every nation and all tribes and
> peoples and tongues, standing before the
> throne and before the Lamb, clothed in
> white robes, and palm branches were in
> their hands; and they cry out with a loud
> voice, saying, "Salvation to our God who
> sits on the throne, and to the Lamb." And
> all the angels were standing around the
> throne and around the elders and the four
> living creatures; and they fell on their faces
> before the throne and worshiped God,
> saying, "Amen, blessing and glory and
> wisdom and thanksgiving and honor and
> power and might, be to our God forever
> and ever Amen. (Rev. 7:9–12)

There is a great multitude from every tribe, nation, and tongue before the throne. They are in heaven. This diverse gathering is united in song and holding palm branches, which is a sign of deliverance. They are praising God for salvation, singing the choruses of worship for God and the Lamb. Then the identity of the multitude is revealed.

> Then one of the elders answered, saying to me, "These who are clothed in the white robes, who are they, and where have they come from?" I said to him, "My lord, you know." And he said to me, "These are the ones who come out of the great tribulation, and they have washed their robes and made them white in the blood of the Lamb. For this reason, they are before the throne of God; and they serve Him day and night in His temple; and He who sits on the throne will spread His tabernacle over them. They will hunger no longer, nor thirst anymore; nor will the sun beat down on them, nor any heat; for the Lamb in the center of the throne will be their shepherd, and will guide them to springs of the water of life; and God will wipe every tear from their eyes." (Rev. 7:13–17)

This great multitude came out of the great tribulation. Given their identity as an innumerable multitude that is now rejoicing, a multitude from every tribe, nation, and tongue. These are the raptured saints of all the ages.[5] They endured and kept the faith because of the blood of the Lamb. Once despised, persecuted, and beaten down by the world, they are now safe and secure from all harm. They will never hunger, thirst, or weep. The Lamb will be their shepherd and guide them to eternal sustenance and satisfaction. God Himself, our Father, will wipe away every tear from their eyes. Indeed, "God has not destined us for wrath, but for obtaining salvation through our Lord Jesus Christ, who died for us, so that whether we are awake or asleep, we will live together with Him" (1 Thess. 5:9–10).

THE TIMING OF THE "GREAT GATHERING"

We do not know the day or hour, or the times or the epochs, of when this great gathering will occur and this wonderful scene will become a reality. However, we have been given the signs of the season. We are to keep watch. We are to be always on the alert so we do not miss the markers Christ and His apostles have laid down for us. The teaching of Christ in the Olivet Discourse, the teaching of Paul in the Thessalonian epistles, and the teaching of John in Revelation all confirm that the great gathering of God's elect will occur at an unknown day and hour after the abomination of desolation and the apostasy occurs.

At the *parousia*, or coming of Christ, the dead in Christ will be raised, those who are alive and remain will be caught up, and we will be with the Lord forever. The Lamb is our eternal shepherd who will guide us to the waters of life. Those who trust in Him will be refreshed and nourished forever.

Paul's Teaching on the Timing Of the Gathering of God's Elect

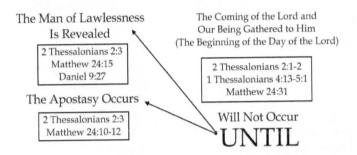

While the redeemed are restored and safely before the throne of God in heaven, where He is wiping away their tears, the inshabitants of the earth have a very different appointment with the King of the Universe. They have spurned His grace, persecuted His people, and blasphemed His Name. We now read further in the book of Revelation to behold the dynamics of the great and terrible Day of the Lord.

End Notes 8

[1] See Tracy L. Howard, "The Literary Unity of 1 Thessalonians 4:13-5:11," *Grace Theological Journal* 9.2 (1988), 163-190, for exposition on the unity of this section of the epistle.

[2] Greek: *tote*

[3] Another variety of partial preterism as popularized by Beasley-Murray (*Jesus and the Last Days* [Peabody: Hendrickson, 1993], 448-449), holds that "all these things" includes everything but the "coming" of the Son of Man, with "all these things" being fulfilled in the first century and Christ's coming remaining yet unfulfilled. However, the parallels between the Thessalonian epistles and the Olivet Discourse already noted render this interpretation untenable.

[4] Since the full preterist denies a future bodily resurrection, both partial preterists and futurists are commonly united in declaring that this denies a necessity of "the faith delivered once for all" and is therefore outside of realm of orthodoxy.

[5] There is a seeming tension between the Olivet Discourse and Revelation in regards to the timing of this gathering. Jesus declares that the gathering of His elect takes place immediately after the tribulation of those days, whereas Revelation indicates that all those before the throne come out of "the Great Tribulation." The tension is relieved when we understand the distinct usage of "tribulation" in these two texts. In the Olivet Discourse, Jesus refers to the *activity* of tribulation. The book of Revelation indicates that the "great tribulation" is described as an *event* consisting of 42 months.

9

THE GREAT AND TERRIBLE DAY OF THE LORD

Understanding What We Are Delivered From

The Lamb holds in His hand the scroll. Initially, there were seven seals—seven preconditions that had to take place before the scroll could be opened and its contents read. Six seals have been broken. There have been false christs, war, famine, death, and martyrdom. When the Lamb broke the sixth seal, the sign of God's divine wrath was revealed. The Lord Jesus Christ returned. Every eye has seen the King of Kings. The people the world hated, killed, and persecuted are now raised, transformed, and safely in heaven with their Father and Lord. The ungodly world is now waiting in terror for what will happen next.

This reflects the reality that Jesus predicted in the Olivet Discourse. In the wake of describing His coming, Jesus teaches that the world will not be ready or expecting His return.

> "For the coming of the Son of Man will be just like the days of Noah. For as in those days before the flood they were eating and drinking, marrying and giving in marriage, until the day that Noah entered the ark, and they did not understand until the flood came and took them all away; so will the coming of the Son of Man be." (Matt. 24:37–39)

Like the days of Noah, the world will be eating, drinking, marrying, and unaware of the reality of coming judgment. The flood came and destroyed everything and everyone except for Noah and his family. Unlike the days of Noah, however, this present world will not be destroyed by water. It will be destroyed by fire. Writes the apostle Peter,

> Know this first of all, that in the last days mockers will come with their mocking, following after their own lusts, and saying, "Where is the promise of His coming? For ever since the fathers fell asleep, all continues just as it was from the beginning of creation." For when they maintain this, it escapes their notice that by the word of God the heavens existed long ago and the earth was formed out of water and by water, through which the world at that time was destroyed, being flooded with water. But by His word the present

> heavens and earth are being reserved for
> fire, kept for the day of judgment and
> destruction of ungodly men . . . But the
> day of the Lord will come like a thief, in
> which the heavens will pass away with a
> roar and the elements will be destroyed
> with intense heat, and the earth and its
> works will be burned up. (1 Pet. 3:3–7, 10)

Understanding these dynamics, we continue the
divine drama in Revelation 8, with the Lamb breaking
the seventh and final seal of the scroll.

> When the Lamb broke the seventh seal,
> there was silence in heaven for about half
> an hour. And I saw the seven angels who
> stand before God, and seven trumpets
> were given to them. Another angel came
> and stood at the altar, holding a golden
> censer; and much incense was given to
> him, so that he might add it to the prayers
> of all the saints on the golden altar which
> was before the throne. And the smoke of
> the incense, with the prayers of the saints,
> went up before God out of the angel's
> hand. Then the angel took the censer and
> filled it with the fire of the altar, and
> threw it to the earth; and there followed
> peals of thunder and sounds and flashes of
> lightning and an earthquake. And the
> seven angels who had the seven trumpets
> prepared themselves to sound them. (Rev.
> 8:1–6)

Once the Lamb breaks the seventh seal, there is
a half-hour silence. It is the calm before the storm.

Seven trumpets are given to seven angels. Trumpets were used in the ancient world as a call to battle. These trumpets signify God's systematic, unstoppable wrath that will be leveled against the world. However, before one trumpet is sounded, the Father allows the saints in heaven to deliver the first blow. Recall the fifth seal. The martyrs cried out to God for justice. They were told to wait. Now their prayers go up before the Father, and His angels throw down thunder, lightning, and an earthquake, breaking the heavenly silence. The seven angels prepare to sound the trumpets of divine war.

THE FIRST SIX TRUMPETS

When we see the nature of the trumpet judgments, there is no mistaking that this is the wrath of Almighty God. Their results are devastating to the earth and those who dwell upon it. Peter declared the elements will "melt with fire and intense heat." The trumpet judgments perfectly fit this description.

TRUMPET ONE: JUDGMENT UPON THE EARTH

> The first sounded, and there came hail and fire, mixed with blood, and they were thrown to the earth; and a third of the earth was burned up, and a third of the trees were burned up, and all the green grass was burned up. (Rev. 8:7)

TRUMPET TWO: JUDGMENT UPON THE SEA

The second angel sounded, and something like a great mountain burning with fire was thrown into the sea; and a third of the sea became blood, and a third of the creatures which were in the sea and had life, died; and a third of the ships were destroyed. (Rev. 8:8–9)

TRUMPET THREE: JUDGMENT UPON THE RIVERS AND SPRINGS

The third angel sounded, and a great star fell from heaven, burning like a torch, and it fell on a third of the rivers and on the springs of waters. The name of the star is called Wormwood; and a third of the waters became wormwood, and many men died from the waters, because they were made bitter. (Rev. 8:10–11)

TRUMPET FOUR: JUDGMENT UPON THE SKIES

The fourth angel sounded, and a third of the sun and a third of the moon and a third of the stars were struck, so that a third of them would be darkened and the day would not shine for a third of it, and the night in the same way. (Rev. 8:12)

TRUMPET FIVE: JUDGMENT OF TORMENT FOR THE INHABITANTS OF THE EARTH

Then the fifth angel sounded, and I saw a star from heaven which had fallen to the earth; and the key of the bottomless pit was given to him. He opened the bottomless pit, and smoke went up out of the pit, like the smoke of a great furnace; and the sun and the air were darkened by the smoke of the pit. Then out of the smoke came locusts upon the earth, and power was given them, as the scorpions of the earth have power. They were told not to hurt the grass of the earth, nor any green thing, nor any tree, but only the men who do not have the seal of God on their foreheads. And they were not permitted to kill anyone, but to torment for five months; and their torment was like the torment of a scorpion when it stings a man. And in those days men will seek death and will not find it; they will long to die, and death flees from them. (Rev. 9:1–6)

TRUMPET SIX: JUDGMENT OF FIERY DEATH TO ONE-THIRD OF MANKIND

Then the sixth angel sounded, and I heard a voice from the four horns of the golden altar which is before God, one saying to the sixth angel who had the trumpet, "Release the four angels who are bound at the great river Euphrates." And the four angels, who had been prepared for the hour and day and month and year, were released, so that they would kill a third of mankind. The number of the armies of the horsemen was two hundred million; I heard the number of them. And this is how I saw in the vision the horses and those who sat on them: the riders had breastplates the color of fire and of hyacinth and of brimstone; and the heads of the horses are like the heads of lions; and out of their mouths proceed fire and smoke and brimstone. A third of mankind was killed by these three plagues, by the fire and the smoke and the brimstone which proceeded out of their mouths. (Rev. 9:13–18)

These plagues are a systematic judgment of all that the earth takes for granted. All areas of creation are destroyed by fire and plagues. The earth, the grass, the sea, the skies, and the earth's inhabitants all experience the initial purging of the world by fire. Even after these woeful plagues have been poured out, the attitude of those who survive will not change. They still will not repent. Much like Pharaoh, their hearts are hardened.

John tells us,

The rest of mankind, who were not killed by these plagues, did not repent of the works of their hands, so as not to worship demons, and the idols of gold and of silver and of brass and of stone and of wood,

which can neither see nor hear nor walk;
and they did not repent of their murders nor
of their sorceries nor of their immorality nor
of their thefts. (Rev. 9:20–21)

THE SIGNIFICANCE OF
THE SEVENTH TRUMPET

Now the seventh trumpet is about to sound.
The significance of this cannot be overstated. This
signals the end of the content of the scroll. The "title
deed" to the kingdom is now enacted. Once the
seventh trumpet is sounded, there is rejoicing.

> Then the seventh angel sounded; and
> there were loud voices in heaven, saying,
> "The kingdom of the world has become
> the kingdom of our Lord and of His
> Christ; and He will reign forever and
> ever." And the twenty-four elders, who sit
> on their thrones before God, fell on their
> faces and worshiped God, saying, "We give
> You thanks, O Lord God, the Almighty,
> who are and who were, because You have
> taken Your great power and have begun to
> reign. (Rev. 11:15–17)

When the seventh trumpet sounds, this world is
claimed as the kingdom of God and His Christ. Two
immensely anticipated events occur at this time: the
reclamation of the world and the "mystery of God" is
finished. Both of these events are intimately related.

Earlier in Revelation, the seventh trumpet is anticipated, citing the significance of what transpires when the angel's last trumpet sounds.

> But in the days of the voice of the seventh angel, when he is about to sound, then the mystery of God is finished, as He preached to His servants the prophets. (Rev. 10:7)

So when the last trumpet sounds, the "mystery of God" is finished. What is the mystery of God? The Old Testament is filled with prophecies regarding the coming of Christ and His kingdom. Book after book is replete with predictions of Messianic prophecy. A King is coming. He is going to judge Israel. He is going to save Israel. He is going to judge the Gentiles. He is going to save the Gentiles. All of these elements are evident in the Old Testament scriptures. However, exactly *how* these prophecies were to be fulfilled was hidden. With the first coming of Christ, the mystery of God, previously unknown, was revealed. In the epistle of Ephesians and the book of Romans, Paul speaks of this mystery.

> By referring to this, when you read you can understand my insight into the mystery of Christ, which in other generations was not made known to the sons of men, as it has now been revealed to His holy apostles and prophets in the Spirit; to be specific, that the Gentiles are fellow heirs and fellow members of the body, and fellow partakers of the promise in Christ Jesus through the gospel, of which I was made a minister, according to the gift of God's

> grace which was given to me according to
> the working of His power. (Eph. 3:4–7)

> For I do not want you, brethren, to be
> uninformed of this mystery—so that you
> will not be wise in your own estimation—
> that a partial hardening has happened to
> Israel until the fullness of the Gentiles has
> come in. (Rom. 11:25)

With the first coming of Christ and the
commission of the gospel, we see that God has caused
a partial hardening to Israel while He gathers Gentiles
into His kingdom. However, this partial hardening
will eventually cease. Recall the 70 sevens. When
history reaches the end of the last seven, Israel will
bring in "everlasting righteousness." All Israel will be
saved. When all Israel is saved, this will mean riches
for the world. Note again Paul's teaching in Romans
11:12:

> Now if their transgression is riches for the
> world and their failure is riches for the
> Gentiles, how much more will their
> fulfillment be!

Here we can see how the events of the seventh
trumpet are intimately related to the mystery of God.
When the seventh trumpet sounds, the mystery of
God is finished. The fullness of the Gentiles has come
in and all Israel is saved. When the seventh trumpet
sounds, the kingdoms of this world are now the
kingdom of our God and His Christ. Israel is saved
and the nations will be blessed by her. With this

being the case, this would put the seventh trumpet right after the end of the 70th seven.

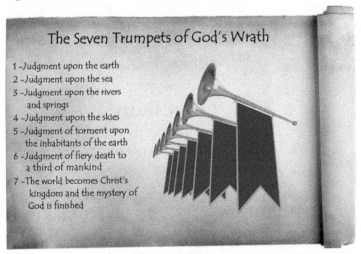

The Seven Trumpets of God's Wrath

1 -Judgment upon the earth
2 -Judgment upon the sea
3 -Judgment upon the rivers and springs
4 -Judgment upon the skies
5 -Judgment of torment upon the inhabitants of the earth
6 -Judgment of fiery death to a third of mankind
7 -The world becomes Christ's kingdom and the mystery of God is finished

Those familiar with Revelation will recognize that there still is much left to happen. There are still seven bowls to be poured out and the final battle of Armageddon is yet to occur. There is an obscure passage at the end of the book of Daniel that may give us insight into this extended period of time.

> "From the time that the regular sacrifice is abolished and the abomination of desolation is set up, there will be 1,290 days." (Dan. 12:11)

Daniel doesn't explicitly state what this 1,290 days is to accomplish. We can ascertain that there is an extension of thirty days for the abomination of desolation. It is this author's view that the Lord allows this extension after the salvation of Israel in order to deal out furious retribution to the "last beast empire," including the Antichrist. These are contained in the bowl judgments. The Greek word for "bowl" indicates a shallow dish that could quickly dispense of its contents. Following the seventh trumpet, the world is now subject to the final stages of the Day of the Lord wrath. With these, the wrath of God is finished.

THE SEVEN BOWLS

THE FIRST BOWL: PAINFUL SORES UPON WORSHIPPERS OF THE BEAST

> Then I heard a loud voice from the temple, saying to the seven angels, "Go and pour out on the earth the seven bowls of the wrath of God." So the first angel went and poured out his bowl on the earth; and it became a loathsome and malignant sore on the people who had the mark of the beast and who worshiped his image. (Rev. 16:1–2)

THE SECOND BOWL: SEAS TURNED TO BLOOD

> The second angel poured out his bowl into the sea, and it became blood like that of a dead man; and every living thing in the sea died. (Rev. 16:3)

THE THIRD BOWL: RIVERS TURNED TO BLOOD

> Then the third angel poured out his bowl into the rivers and the springs of waters; and they became blood. And I heard the angel of the waters saying, "Righteous are

You, who are and who were, O Holy One,
because You judged these things; for they
poured out the blood of saints and
prophets, and You have given them blood
to drink. They deserve it." And I heard
the altar saying, "Yes, O Lord God, the
Almighty, true and righteous are Your
judgments." (Rev. 16:4–7)

THE FOURTH BOWL: SCORCHING FIRE ON INHABITANTS OF EARTH

The fourth angel poured out his bowl upon
the sun, and it was given to it to scorch
men with fire. Men were scorched with
fierce heat; and they blasphemed the
name of God who has the power over these
plagues, and they did not repent so as to
give Him glory. (Rev. 16:8–9)

THE FIFTH BOWL: THE BEAST'S KINGDOM DARKENED

Then the fifth angel poured out his bowl
on the throne of the beast, and his
kingdom became darkened; and they
gnawed their tongues because of pain, and
they blasphemed the God of heaven
because of their pains and their sores; and
they did not repent of their deeds. (Rev.
16:10–11)

THE SIXTH BOWL: THE WAY PREPARED FOR ARMAGEDDON

The sixth angel poured out his bowl on the
great river, the Euphrates; and its water

was dried up, so that the way would be prepared for the kings from the east. And I saw coming out of the mouth of the dragon and out of the mouth of the beast and out of the mouth of the false prophet, three unclean spirits like frogs; for they are spirits of demons, performing signs, which go out to the kings of the whole world, to gather them together for the war of the great day of God, the Almighty. ("Behold, I am coming like a thief. Blessed is the one who stays awake and keeps his clothes, so that he will not walk about naked and men will not see his shame.") And they gathered them together to the place which in Hebrew is called Har-Magedon. (Rev. 16:12–16)

THE SEVENTH BOWL: GREATEST EARTHQUAKE OF ALL TIME, GREAT HAILSTORM

Then the seventh angel poured out his bowl upon the air, and a loud voice came out of the temple from the throne, saying, "It is done." And there were flashes of lightning and sounds and peals of thunder; and there was a great earthquake, such as there had not been since man came to be upon the earth, so great an earthquake was it, and so mighty. The great city was split into three parts, and the cities of the nations fell. Babylon the great was remembered before God, to give her the cup of the wine of His fierce wrath. And every island fled away, and the mountains were not found. And huge hailstones, about one hundred pounds each, came down from heaven upon men; and men blasphemed God because of the plague of the hail, because its plague was extremely severe. (Rev. 16:17–21)

With the last bowl, we hear the declaration, "It is done." The wrath of God is complete. It is interesting to note the parallels between the bowl judgments and the judgments displayed during the Exodus. The kingdom of Pharaoh and Egypt is considered to be the first beast empire.[1] (A "beast empire" is one that campaigns against the purposes and people of God.) During the time of the Exodus, Pharaoh and his kingdom persecuted the people of God. God delivered His people from Egypt and displayed His power through signs and wonders, demonstrating He is the Lord of all creation. Recall that before the bowls are poured out, Israel will have been saved. They will be saved and protected, and as with the first beast empire (Egypt), the last beast empire (Antichrist's kingdom) will experience God's furious wrath for mistreating and opposing His people and purposes. Note below the parallels between the bowls judgments and the plagues that occurred during the Exodus.

God's systematic destruction of the last beast empire will come to its climax at the battle of Armageddon. Like Pharaoh, through all these plagues, the hearts of the world will be hardened. Rather than repent, they will blaspheme the Almighty.

The Destruction of the First "Beast Empire"	The Destruction of the Last "Beast Empire"
•Water Turned to Blood (Exodus 7:20-21)	•Water Turned to Blood (Revelation 16:3-4)
•Painful Sores on the People (Exodus 9:8)	•Painful Sores on the People (Revelation 16:2)
•A Great Hailstorm (Exodus 9:22-25)	•A Great Hailstorm (Revelation 16:21)
•Darkness Over All the Land (Exodus 10:21-22)	•Darkness Over All the Land (Revelation 16:10)
•The Sea Turned into Dry Land to Judge the Armies (Exodus 14:21-28)	•The River Turned into Dry Land to Judge the Armies (Revelation 16:12-14)

THE BATTLE OF ARMAGEDDON

When we arrive at Revelation 19, we read of the great battle of the ages. The whole world gathers in the Valley of Megiddo, also known as Armageddon, to wage war against the Lord and His Christ. It is this writer's belief that this event takes place at the time of the seventh bowl. For at the time of the pouring of the seventh bowl, it is declared that the wrath of God is finished. In Revelation 17–19, we are taken into greater detail on what transpires within this "finishing wrath of God." At the seventh bowl, Babylon, the beast, and all who wage war with him are resoundingly defeated by the King of Kings and Lord of Lords.

> And I saw heaven opened, and behold, a white horse, and He who sat on it is called Faithful and True, and in righteousness He judges and wages war. His eyes are a flame of fire, and on His head are many diadems; and He has a name written on Him which no one knows except Himself. He is clothed with a robe dipped in blood, and His name is called The Word of God. And the armies which are in heaven, clothed in fine linen, white and clean, were following Him on white horses. From His mouth comes a sharp sword, so that with it He may strike down the nations, and He will rule them with a rod of iron; and He treads the wine press of the fierce wrath of God, the Almighty. And on His robe and on His thigh He has a name written, "KING OF KINGS, AND LORD OF LORDS." (Rev. 19:11–16)

There is a striking contrast at the time of the Battle of Armageddon. Those who are Christ's are told to make themselves ready, for the Marriage Supper of the Lamb is upon them (Rev. 19:7–9). The redeemed are still safe with the King in heaven. They are told to prepare for the great banquet. They are going to feast with Abraham, Isaac, and Jacob. All those who are redeemed by the blood of the Lamb will recline with each other, fixing their eyes on Jesus, the author and finisher of their salvation. For those aligned with the Antichrist, another feast is planned:

> Then I saw an angel standing in the sun,
> and he cried out with a loud voice, saying
> to all the birds which fly in midheaven,
> "Come, assemble for the great supper of
> God, so that you may eat the flesh of kings
> and the flesh of commanders and the flesh
> of mighty men and the flesh of horses and
> of those who sit on them and the flesh of
> all men, both free men and slaves, and
> small and great." And I saw the beast and
> the kings of the earth and their armies
> assembled to make war against Him who
> sat on the horse and against His army.
> And the beast was seized, and with him
> the false prophet who performed the signs
> in his presence, by which he deceived
> those who had received the mark of the
> beast and those who worshiped his image;
> these two were thrown alive into the lake
> of fire which burns with brimstone. And
> the rest were killed with the sword which
> came from the mouth of Him who sat on
> the horse, and all the birds were filled
> with their flesh. (Rev. 19:17–21)

The irony is thick. God's children will be entering
eternal delight at the Marriage Feast of the Lamb, while
the wicked will be food for the birds of prey. Here we
read of the end of the Antichrist, the false prophet, and
all those who aligned themselves with them for a futile
battle against the King of Kings. Paul declares this
destruction this way: "Then that lawless one will be
revealed whom the Lord will slay with the breath of His

mouth and bring to an end by the appearance of His coming [*parousia*]" (2 Thess. 2:8).

UNDERSTANDING THE "PAROUSIA" OF JESUS CHRIST

With the rapture of the church, the wrath of God, and the defeat of nations and the beast at the battle of Armageddon now in our expositional hindsight, we can ask, "How do we best understand the *parousia* of Jesus Christ? Is there a second and third coming of Christ?" We need to look closer at the term *parousia* to better understand this point.

As already mentioned, the Greek word *parousia* is a noun. It describes an event (although actions are implied). Within this one event, many sub-actions may occur.

To clarify, let's consider the first *parousia* of Christ. His first coming was an extended singular event (thirty-plus years) that consisted of many parts, including His virgin birth, His working of miracles, His teaching, His death, His resurrection, and His ascension. Likewise, His second *parousia* will be a singular event consisting of many parts, including His appearing in the sky, His rapturing and raising the elect, His pouring out of grace upon Israel, His pouring out of wrath, and His triumph at the battle of Armageddon.

Therefore, there will *not* be a second and third coming of Christ. Rather, there will be a future singular *parousia* event that consists of many components. The coming *parousia* is virtually synonymous with the Day of the Lord. At this time, the righteous will be vindicated, Israel will be purged and refined, the nations will be judged, and the kingdoms of this world will become the kingdom of our God and His Christ.

DESTINED FOR SALVATION

As we have seen, the Day of the Lord is a terrifying event. It is the day when God unleashes His furious anger upon those who oppose Him. God's wrath is coming. God's wrath is sure. God's wrath is real. Those who believe in the person and work of Jesus Christ are destined for deliverance from this wrath. In the context of his teachings regarding the day of the Lord, the apostle Paul proclaims, "For God has not destined us for wrath, but for obtaining salvation through our Lord Jesus Christ" (1 Thess. 5:9).

We are destined to obtain salvation and deliverance from the wrath of God and the Lamb. This day will be terrible for the wicked world, but will be vindication for all who trust in Him to deliver them and distribute justice. As constituents of the kingdom of God who are now living in a foreign land, we do well to call to mind the impending reality of that day. As the apostle Peter exhorts us:

> Since all these things are to be destroyed in this way, what sort of people ought you to be in holy conduct and godliness? (2 Pet. 3:11)

150

End Notes 9

[1] See Robert Van Kampen, *The Sign of Christ's Coming and the End of the Age* (Wheaton: Crossway, 1999), 101-116, for a study on the first seven beast empires.

THE PARABLE OF THE FIG TREE

10

What About Imminence?

Answering the Question,
"Could Christ Come at Any Moment?"

A s you have been reading this book, a nagging question may have tugged at your mind: "Doesn't the Bible declare that Jesus could come at any moment?" The first nine chapters of this book have been built on biblical exposition of the Olivet Discourse, the book of Daniel, the Thessalonian epistles, and the book of Revelation. The conclusion has been that clear, distinguishable signs will herald the return of Christ. This is the point of the parable of the fig tree. When the signs prophesied by Jesus come to pass, we are to recognize He is near, right at the door. This teaching clashes with the belief that Christ could return at any moment, perhaps even today. This belief is known by many as *imminence.*

DEFINING IMMINENCE

Before engaging the contemporary doctrine of imminence, we must wrestle with the definition of this term. Imminence, in its simplest definition, is an overhanging event that is threatening to arrive. However, in modern eschatology, the term has morphed to mean that Christ could return for His church *at any moment.* Those who adhere to this sense of imminence assert that Christ's coming for His church need not be preceded by any signs and thus could occur at any time. Obviously, this concept greatly conflicts with what has been asserted in the book. Because any-moment imminence is such a popular doctrine and is held with vigorous passion by many, we need to carefully consider the arguments and usage of scripture in support of this position. Since the Bible is consistent in its teaching, either any-moment imminence is flawed or the command to watch for the signs of the fig tree does not apply to us. Let's take a closer look at the arguments for any-moment imminence and see whether they pass the tests of sound biblical exposition.

ARGUMENT FOR IMMINENCE #1: NO ONE KNOWS THE DAY OR THE HOUR

The most common argument I have heard for an "any moment" return of Christ is that no man knows the day or the hour of His return. This argument fails because it ignores the immediate context of the passage. Jesus' proclamation that "no man knows the day or the hour" comes on the heels of His teaching in the Olivet Discourse. As has been demonstrated, clear signs precede the coming described in Matthew 24. Furthermore, while "no man knows the day or the hour," we are commanded to know the season of the Lord's return. This teaching is given in the very context of the parable itself.

> "Now learn the parable from the fig tree: when its branch has already become tender and puts forth its leaves, you know that summer is near; so, you too, when you see all these things, recognize that He is near, right at the door. Truly I say to you, this generation will not pass away until all these things take place. Heaven and earth will pass away, but My words will not pass away. But of that day and hour no one knows, not even the angels of heaven, nor the Son, but the Father alone." (Matt. 24:32–36)

Therefore, Jesus' teaching is clarified when we put it in its proper context. No man knows the day or the hour. Church history has proven this to be so. Prophetic pretenders have continually arisen, claiming to know the exact date or time, and have been proven false. However, Jesus Himself tells us that when the signs that He outlined in the Olivet Discourse take place, we are to "know He is near, right at the door." Even so, the exact day and hour will remain unknown until it arrives.

Therefore, when we look at the context of the teaching that no one knows that day or hour, we see that this *in no way* teaches any-moment imminence. In fact, quite the opposite is true. Distinguishable signs will precede the return of Jesus Christ for His people.

ARGUMENT FOR IMMINENCE #2: THE LORD WILL COME LIKE A THIEF IN THE NIGHT

Another common argument for any-moment imminence is the teaching that the Lord will come "like a thief in the night" (1 Thess. 5:2). According to this argument, since the coming of the Lord will be sudden and surprising, this implies that He may come at any moment. Before considering the merit of this argument, we need to understand the imagery Jesus is using. When Jesus declares that He is coming like a thief (a comparison also seen in the Thessalonian epistles and the book of Revelation), it indeed declares that His coming will be surprising and unexpected. A thief attempts to come in the night when no one is watching or expecting it. However, this does not imply any-moment imminence. Here is why.

When Jesus uses this imagery, it is in the context of the Olivet Discourse, where the only "coming" He has announced is the one in the midst of the great tribulation, when He shuts down all natural light and returns in glory. It is in this context in which the Lord returns. Beyond this, Jesus' coming like a thief will be only for those who are unprepared.

Those who are faithful will recognize the signs of the times and endure, waiting expectantly for the return of their King. It is only those who have aligned themselves with the world and its ruler who will be surprised and unprepared. Consider Paul's instruction in 1 Thessalonians:

> Now as to the times and the epochs, brethren, you have no need of anything to be written to you. For you yourselves know full well that the day of the Lord will come just like a thief in the night. While they are saying, "Peace and safety!" then destruction will come upon them suddenly like labor pains upon a woman with child, and they will not escape. *But you, brethren, are not in darkness, that the day would overtake you like a thief*; for you are all sons of light and sons of day. We are not of night nor of darkness; so then let us not sleep as others do, but let us be alert and sober. (1 Thess. 5:1–6, emphasis added)

Therefore, the Lord's coming "like a thief" does not imply any-moment imminence. Rather, this surprising and sudden terrifying reality will strike those who are unprepared at His return.

ARGUMENT FOR IMMINENCE #3:
THE COMING OF THE LORD IS "NEAR"

Many point to James 5 as proof of any-moment imminence.

> Therefore be patient, brethren, until the
> coming of the Lord. The farmer waits for
> the precious produce of the soil, being
> patient about it, until it gets the early and
> late rains. You too be patient; strengthen
> your hearts, for the coming [*parousia*] of the
> Lord is near. (James 5:7–8)

Those holding to any-moment imminence assert that if the "Lord is near," no signs need to occur before His return. However, upon closer biblical examination this implication is demonstrated to be in error.

The Greek word for "near" is *eggiken*. This term is likely being used to allude to the resurrection and ascension of Christ and the spread of the gospel, which create the present anticipation of the next great event in salvation history—His *parousia*. In fact, this same root of this Greek term was used to describe the feasts in the Gospels: "Now the Passover of the Jews was near [*eggus*], and many went up to Jerusalem out of the country before the Passover to purify themselves" (John 11:55). Obviously, the Passover was not going to occur at any moment. On the contrary, the Passover, which had a fixed day, had drawn near because of a past action (the completion of the last feast), thus creating the present result (the anticipation for the next feast, Passover). Therefore, this is confirming evidence that the declaration "the Lord is near" does not imply an any-moment coming of Christ.[1]

ARGUMENT FOR IMMINENCE #4: THE RESTRAINER MUST BE REMOVED

Many believe that the Bible declares that the church is the "restrainer" of the man of lawlessness. According to this line of reasoning, once God removes the church (via the rapture), the man of lawlessness is revealed. In this thinking, the removal of the restrainer (the church) is imminent. A glaring problem with this thinking is that the Bible *nowhere* indicates this as the case. The Bible does declare that there is someone and something restraining the man of lawlessness, but in no way does it declare that the church is this restraining influence.

Here is the text at issue:

> And you know what restrains him now, so that in his time he will be revealed. For the mystery of lawlessness is already at work; only he who now restrains will do so until he is taken out of the way. (2 Thess. 2:6–7)

Several solid suggestions have been offered to the identity of this restrainer.[2] However, we must humbly confess that the scriptures *do not* explicitly identify him. Yet, of all the entities this restrainer could be, one particular entity is excluded—the church.

Taking 2 Thessalonians 2:1–8 as a cohesive whole, we read that the coming of the Lord and our being gathered to Him (the beginning of the Day of the Lord, as confirmed in 1 Thessalonians 4–5 and the sixth seal of Revelation) cannot happen until the man of lawlessness is revealed and the apostasy occurs. *If* "the coming of our Lord and our being gathered to Him" (the rapture of the church) cannot occur until after the "man of lawlessness" is revealed; and *if* the restrainer is removed prior to this revealing; *then* it is impossible for the church to be the restrainer *since* "the coming of the Lord and our being gathered to Him" happens after the restrainer is removed.

The Restrainer Removed

Paul's Teaching on the Order of End Times Events in 2 Thessalonians 2:1-8

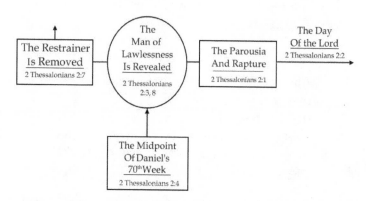

In light of these considerations, identifying the church as the restrainer is untenable and does not support an "any moment" coming of Jesus Christ.

ARGUMENT FOR IMMINENCE #5:
WE WILL BE "KEPT FROM THE HOUR"

Revelation 3:10 offers a promise: "Because you have kept my word of perseverance, I will also keep you from the hour of trial that is about to come upon the whole earth." Many have taken this promise to mean that the rapture will occur before "the tribulation" starts, this making the coming of Christ imminent. However, there are a couple of interpretive factors that nullify this view.

Revelation 2–3 contains Jesus' exhortations and admonitions to the seven churches in Asia Minor. We must ask, "How do these letters fit into the prophetic message of Revelation?" I believe the best way to understand these instructions is to recognize the near/far implications of prophecy. These letters commissioned by Jesus Christ were given to seven literal churches that existed at the end of the first century. This is the "near" application of these letters. However, we must well remember that the book of Revelation's primary message is that of the consummation of all things. Therefore, these seven churches also embody the various states of the church in general at the time of the end.[3] Because the underlying issues evident in these letters transcend time, the messages given by Christ to His church are also to be read, understood, and heeded by His people throughout the age of the church. In my mind, this is the only viable way to preserve the historical, prophetic, and continuing function of the letters of Revelation 2–3.

With the above being the case, how does the promise of preservation from the hour of trial fit into the framework of Revelation? A careful reading of these letters reveals that two churches were faithful (Smyrna, Philadelphia), four were compromising (Ephesus, Thyatira, Pergamum, Laodicia), and one was dead (Sardis). The compromising churches were commanded to repent or face severe discipline. The dead church was called to repent or face divine wrath. Notice that, while both Smyrna and Philadelphia were faithful to the King, they were given starkly different destinies. One was told of coming persecution and tribulation (Smyrna). The other was promised to be kept from this time of trial (Philadelphia).

So how does this expand our understanding of being "kept from the hour"? I believe the hour of trial is the Great Tribulation. This time is going to test the whole world to see where one's allegiance lies: with Christ or with the Antichrist. A portion of the church of Christ will have already passed the test. We don't know who these people will be, but Christ will. And since they have "kept His command to persevere," they will not be subjected to the testing of the tribulation fires. This is a sovereign decision of Christ that may well be His means of having a multitude that "remains" when He returns. While this time will affect every tribe, nation, and tongue, Christ will supernaturally keep a portion of His people from this trial for His own purposes.

Note, too, that "kept from" does not necessitate *removal*. In like manner, Jesus prays for His people to be "kept from" the evil one. But this does not entail removal from the earth.

> "I have given them Your word; and the world has hated them, because they are not of the world, even as I am not of the world. I do not ask You to take them out of the world, but to keep them from the evil one." (John 17:14–15)

Thus, being kept from the hour of trial does not indicate an imminent removal from the earth, but rather *protection* of a portion of the church from the time of trial because of previous perseverance and the purposes of God.

ARGUMENT FOR IMMINENCE #6: THE 70TH WEEK IS FOR ISRAEL, NOT THE CHURCH

One argument for imminence comes from a theological paradigm that insists that God works with Israel and the church in different dispensations with little to no overlap. According to this argument, since the first 69 sevens were focused on Israel, then the 70th must be, as well. In this paradigm, since the church is not present in the 70th seven, then the rapture is imminent.

It is true that the 70th seven focuses very much on the both the land and people of Israel. However, it is erroneous to believe that God has not, and will not, deal with Israel and the church at the same time. First, the church did not exist during the first 69 sevens, so to say that God will not deal with the church in the 70th seven because He didn't during the first 69 is stretching the bounds of sound reasoning. Second, we must insist that God *has been* working with both Israel and the church since she was born on Pentecost. God has been saving a remnant of Israel during the age of the church. God has been disciplining Israel during the age of the church. God has brought Israel back into her own land during the age of the church. History confirms that the Almighty has no difficulty dealing with both Israel and the church at the same time. We can expect the same when the 70th seven unfolds on the scene of history. In His sovereign wisdom and mercy, the Almighty will consummate His work with both Israel and the church during the 70th seven to the praise and glory of His grace.

ARGUMENT FOR IMMINENCE: #7: WE ARE TO LOOK FOR CHRIST, NOT THE ANTICHRIST

An example of not being able to see the forest through the trees is the argument that we are commanded to look for Christ and not the Antichrist. Therefore, Christ's coming must be imminent.

There are two glaring errors here. First, we *are* commanded to look for the Antichrist. In the Olivet Discourse, Jesus exhorts us to take action and be on the alert when we see the abomination of desolation.

This is a sign to recognize that Christ is near. Paul confirms this in 2 Thessalonians when he declares that the man of lawlessness must be revealed before the Day of the Lord. The revealing of the Antichrist is one of the buds of the fig tree, signaling that Christ's return is near—right at the door.

The other error of this argument is that it does not distinguish between "watching to discern" and "eagerly expecting." We should be looking for the Antichrist in order to discern the perilous time that accompanies his arrival and anticipate the coming of Christ. However, we are not "eagerly expecting" him. The Antichrist's coming is not one that Christians are longing for. We *are* eagerly waiting for Christ's coming. Paul notes in Titus that we are to be "looking for the blessed hope and the appearing of the glory of our great God and Savior, Christ Jesus" (Titus 2:13). In the Greek, "looking" here indicates a longing expectation for, an eager reception. When Jesus appears, we will be raised, grace will be given, and justice will be served. We long to see our Lord and to live with Him forever. This does not imply any-moment imminence. Nor does the fact that tribulation precedes this day diminish our eager expectation. In fact, it *increases it*. It is our "happy hope" that shines in the midst of darkness.

The Illustrations of Matthew 24 in Context

29"But immediately after the tribulation of those days THE SUN WILL BE DARKENED, AND THE MOON WILL NOT GIVE ITS LIGHT, AND THE STARS WILL FALL from the sky, and the powers of the heavens will be shaken. 30"And then the sign of the Son of Man will appear in the sky, and then all the tribes of the earth will mourn, and they will see the SON OF MAN COMING ON THE CLOUDS OF THE SKY with power and great glory. 31"And He will send forth His angels with A GREAT TRUMPET and THEY WILL GATHER TOGETHER His elect from the four winds, from one end of the sky to the other. 32"Now learn the parable from the fig tree: when its branch has already become tender and puts forth its leaves, you know that summer is near; 33so, you too, when you see all these things, recognize that He is near, right at the door. 34 "Truly I say to you, this generation will not pass away until all these things take place. 35"Heaven and earth will pass away, but My words will not pass away. 36"But of that day and hour no one knows, not even the angels of heaven, nor the Son, but the Father alone. 37"For the coming of the Son of Man will be just like the days of Noah. 38"For as in those days before the flood they were eating and drinking, marrying and giving in marriage, until the day that Noah entered the ark, 39and they did not understand until the flood came and took them all away; so will the coming of the Son of Man be. 40"Then there will be two men in the field; one will be taken and one will be left. 41"Two women will be grinding at the mill; one will be taken and one will be left. 42"Therefore be on the alert, for you do not know which day your Lord is coming. 43"But be sure of this, that if the head of the house had known at what time of the night the thief was coming, he would have been on the alert and would not have allowed his house to be broken into. 44"For this reason you also must be ready; for the Son of Man is coming at an hour when you do not think He will.

ARGUMENT FOR IMMINENCE #8: JESUS' ILLUSTRATIONS IN THE OLIVET DISCOURSE IMPLY IMMINENCE

Many read the end-times illustrations in Matthew 24 and conclude that these parables require a belief in any-moment imminence. Before addressing these conclusions, I once again am compelled to remind the reader of the importance of context. The illustrations of Matthew 24 come on the heels of Jesus' primary teaching in the Olivet Discourse. The only "coming" that Jesus taught is His coming in the sky after the signs He outlines. There is a clear connection of terms in this passage that confirms that the illustrations and parables that follow are linked to this coming.

Before explaining the meaning of the two illustrations at issue here, we do well to restrain ourselves when interpreting illustrations and parables. Often times, we are tempted to turn parables into allegories, with every element of the parable holding a secret meaning. However, parables in the Gospels do not function in this manner, and history has demonstrated that treating them this way often produces all sorts of theological error.

For His first illustration, immediately after declaring that the coming of the Son of Man will be as the days of Noah, Jesus teaches the following:

> "Then there will be two men in the field;
> one will be taken and one will be left.
> Two women will be grinding at the mill;
> one will be taken and one will be left."
> (Matt. 24:40–41)

Advocates of any-moment imminence see this as supporting their position since the *parousia* is unexpected. Once again, however, the context demands this must be referring to the results of the coming described in Matthew 24:30–31. So what does this illustration actually teach us regarding the nature of the second coming?

In this text, we discover both a parallel and a contrast to the judgment of the flood. When Christ returns, the elect will be taken to Him for safety from God's wrath, just as Noah and his family were preserved from God's wrath in the Ark.[4] Those who are not taken are left to receive God's justice. However, unlike the times of Noah, salvation will not be a "family matter." At the time of the flood, Noah, his wife, his three sons, and their wives, were saved

167

from God's wrath. At the time of Christ's return, however, members of the same household may have drastically different destinies. The elements of this illustration, millwork and fieldwork, were activities that were engaged in by family members. Most households would have had their own mills to grind grains, and field work was often the family source of income. Therefore, this illustration teaches that, when the Lord returns, salvation will not be a family or clan issue. Rather, it will be if one trusts in the person and work of Jesus Christ.

The next illustration in the Olivet Discourse teaches the importance of continual watching in light of this reality.

> "Therefore be on the alert, for you do not know which day your Lord is coming. But be sure of this, that if the head of the house had known at what time of the night the thief was coming, he would have been on the alert and would not have allowed his house to be broken into. For this reason you also must be ready; for the Son of Man is coming at an hour when you do not think He will." (Matt. 24:42–44)

A thief comes at an unknown hour. Christ has taught us that we do not know when He will return, but He has commanded us to continually watch. This means that we are to always have the expectation of His return. Even though it may not occur in our lifetimes, we still need to stand watch and expect it. To lose this expectation is dangerous. Jesus made this clear in His very next parable.

"Who then is the faithful and sensible slave whom his master put in charge of his household to give them their food at the proper time? Blessed is that slave whom his master finds so doing when he comes. Truly I say to you that he will put him in charge of all his possessions. But if that evil slave says in his heart, 'My master is not coming for a long time, and begins to beat his fellow slaves and eat and drink with drunkards; the master of that slave will come on a day when he does not expect him and at an hour which he does not know, and will cut him in pieces and assign him a place with the hypocrites; in that place there will be weeping and gnashing of teeth." (Matt. 24:45–51)

The one who loses sight of the reality of the Lord's return will fall into wickedness. This is why we always must keep watch. If we don't, we may fall into deception, and His coming may come upon us like a trap.

Of particular interest is the verse, "For this reason you must also be ready, for the Son of Man is coming at an hour you do not think [*dokeite*] He will" (24:44.) This passage is often brought up to support the view that Jesus could come at any moment. Some would state, "How can He come when I don't 'expect' or 'think He will,' if, when I see the signs, I am to know that He is near?" This is a good question that needs a satisfactory answer.

I believe Matthew 24:44 suffers from a deficient translation (in many instances). The deficiency revolves around the word "expect" or "think." Most translations imply that faithful believers will not be expecting Christ when He returns. Some translations even read that He will come when we "least" expect.[5] A New Testament word study of the Greek *dokeo*, which is translated "expect" or "think," produces informative results. Note the following examples from the book of Matthew:

> "Do not suppose [*dokte*] that you can say to yourselves, 'We have Abraham for our father; for I say to you that from these stones God is able to raise up children to Abraham." (Matt. 3:9)

> "When you are praying, do not use meaningless repetition as the Gentiles do, for they suppose [*dokousin*] that they will be heard for their many words." (Matt. 6:7)

> "What do you think [*dokei*] about the Christ, whose son is He?" They said to Him, "The son of David." (Matt. 22:42)

The Greek word *dokeo* denotes an opinion or supposition.[6] If we take the word *dokeite* (to have the opinion) and consider this verb with the negation *ou* (not), this would mean "to have the opinion He is not coming." Given the prior context (the Olivet Discourse, which calls us to expect His coming) and the illustration immediately following (the parable of the unjust servant who has the opinion "my master is not coming for a long time"), this phrase is not a statement of fact, but rather *a warning*.

I believe the best translation that fits the usage of *dokeo* and the context would be, "For the hour that you hold the opinion 'not,' the son of Man comes." Although it is grammatically awkward, it captures the essence of Jesus' warning.[7] It is proverbial, for the hour the watchman becomes lazy and does not think the thief is coming, it is that hour that the thief will come and plunder. Therefore, he must remain watchful *at all times*. In the same way, we are warned, if we lose our expectation and say, "My master is not coming for a long time," we may become deceived and then He *will come* when we suppose "He is not coming."

This warning has a function for all throughout church history, but especially for those who endure the time of the end. Under such harsh and trying conditions as those that will accompany the great tribulation, the temptation will be great to abandon our expectation of Christ's return and join the world and its deceitful pleasures. Those who lose their expectation of the coming of Christ will fall into deception and wickedness and will not escape when He returns.

This function is brought out clearly in Luke's end-times discourse: "Be on guard, so that your hearts will not be weighted down with dissipation and drunkenness and the worries of life, and that day will not come on you suddenly like a trap; for it will come upon all those who dwell on the face of all the earth"

171

(Luke 21:34–35). Those who remain in the hope of Christ's coming are sanctified and that day will not come upon them like a trap. Rather, transformation will transpire. As we read in 1 John 3: "Beloved, now we are children of God, and it has not appeared as yet what we will be. We know that when He appears, we will be like Him, because we will see Him just as He is. And everyone who has this hope fixed on Him purifies himself, just as He is pure" (1 John 3:2–3).

A PHANTOM DOCTRINE

Given the strong biblical evidence confirming that certain signs must precede the return of Christ for His people, coupled with the expository and logical weaknesses of arguments for any-moment imminence, we are compelled to conclude that any-moment imminence is a phantom doctrine.[8] When passages are proclaimed out of context and arguments are made with little to no biblical support, it gives this doctrine the appearance of support, but in actuality, it is nothing more than a doctrinal apparition.

End Notes 10

---

[1] See Robert Gundry, *The Church and the Tribulation* (Grand Rapids: Zondervan, 1973), 32–33, for further commentary on this issue.

[2] Two in particular: 1) Michael the archangel and his legions of righteous angels, and 2) God through the multiple civil authorities.

[3] End-times terminology and imagery throughout the exhortations and admonitions to the seven churches support this. See Revelation 2:22, 3:3.

[4] There has been considerable debate as to whether it is the one "taken" or the one "left" who is judged. Some have pointed to the reference to the ones judged in the flood being "taken away" and suggested this indicates that the ones "taken" are judged. Yet, distinct Greek words are used here which nullify that link. Two factors support the position that the one "taken" is saved and the one "left" is judged. First, in the immediate context, Jesus sends His angels to "gather" His elect. Therefore, the immediate context describes the saved being "taken." Also, the Greek word for "taken" (*paralambano*) is often used to describe the receiving of one to another. It is the same Greek word used in John 14:3: "If I go and prepare a place for you, I will come again and receive (*paralambano*) you to Myself, that where I am, there you may be also."

[5] *The New Living Translation* erroneously translates this term "least expect."

[6] I believe translating this word as "expect" is not warranted here and leads to potential misunderstanding. Elsewhere, Matthew's

usage is of this word is consistently and rightly translated "think" or "suppose."

[7] The *King James Version* and *Green's Literal Translation* closely match this.

[8] Robert Van Kampen, Charles Cooper, *Imminency: The Phantom Doctrine* (Grand Haven: Sola Scriptura, 2000), 1–2.

11

THIS GENERATION WILL
NOT PASS AWAY *UNTIL* . . .

The Olivet Discourse and the Salvation of Israel

"Truly I say to you this generation [*genea*]
will not pass away until all these things
take place." (Matt. 24:34)

Matthew 24:34 has puzzled biblical and
interpretive commentators for generations
(pardon the pun). This passage has resulted
in people declaring that the Bible is in error (e.g.
liberalism), in declarations that Jesus has already
returned (e.g. preterism), and produced a number of
date-setters (e.g. various aberrational sects). It is ironic
that a passage that has been used to attempt to
discredit the Word of God and grossly misinterpret
the Olivet Discourse actually sings of God's
faithfulness and power to preserve His promises.

Allow me to first outline the two primary ways
this passage has been interpreted throughout church

history. Then we will look at the immediate and broader biblical context of the term "this generation." With these accomplished, we will be ready to behold the profound meaning that "this generation will not pass away until all these things take place."

TWO TRADITIONAL INTERPRETATIONS (PRETERIST AND FUTURIST)

The history of biblical interpretation has viewed the phrase "this generation" in two different ways. Preterists assert that "this generation" speaks of a time frame (typically either forty or sixty years) that was already in process at the time Jesus gave the Olivet Discourse. Since preterists believe that the Olivet Discourse (including the "coming" of Christ) is speaking of the destruction of Jerusalem, they believe this prophecy was fulfilled in A.D. 70 when Jerusalem was destroyed by the Roman armies.

For their part, futurists believe that the Olivet Discourse speaks of the time just prior, and including, the return of Jesus Christ. Typically, futurists believe "this generation" speaks of the current or future generation that sees the signs that Jesus outlines in the Olivet Discourse. Many people believed that the fig tree in Matthew 24 represents Israel, and therefore the rebirth of Israel in 1948 signaled the "budding" that promised Christ's return. Since forty years is the commonly held time for "a generation," many thought that Jesus would return within forty years of the rebirth of Israel. This is why 1988 was such a prominent year for date setters of Christ's return.

Yet, all of the above interpretations fail to take important contextual evidence into consideration. It is my conviction that viewing "this generation" as a time frame reference violates the primary usage of this term in the New Testament. Let's examine the dynamics of this term in the Gospels and beyond, then assess from this its most compelling biblical definition.

THE TERM "THIS GENERATION"

To begin, let's examine the most immediate context in the book of Matthew. Just prior to the Olivet Discourse, Matthew records Jesus' words of condemnation to the Jewish leadership of His day.

> "Fill up, then, the measure of the guilt of your fathers. You serpents, you brood of vipers, how will you escape the sentence of hell? Therefore, behold, I am sending you prophets and wise men and scribes; some of them you will kill and crucify, and some of them you will scourge in your synagogues, and persecute from city to city, so that upon you may fall the guilt of all the righteous blood shed on earth, from the blood of righteous Abel to the blood of Zechariah, the son of Berechiah, whom you murdered between the temple and the altar. Truly I say to you, all these things will come upon this generation [genea]." (Matt. 23:32–36)

Here Jesus speaks of the blood of the martyrs being placed upon "this generation," a statement that was directed at the Jewish leadership. So note here "this generation" has a *negative connotation* and is directed at *unbelieving Israelites.*

Jesus uses the term again in Matthew 16:4: "An evil and adulterous generation [*genea*] seeks after a sign; and a sign will not be given it, except the sign of Jonah.' And He left them, and went away." Peter uses it in his sermon in Acts, as well. After the "sign of Jonah" was given (Jesus' death and resurrection), Peter proclaimed the gospel: "And with many other words he solemnly testified and kept on exhorting them, saying, "Be saved from this perverse generation [*geneas*]!" (Acts 2:20). Was Peter telling them to be saved from a time frame? Or was He telling them to be saved from their ungodly condition (those who oppose God's purposes)? The latter is much more compelling.

The fact is that "this generation," the portion of the natural descendants of Abraham, Isaac, and Jacob who grumble and disbelieve in God's promises and power, have been around since the time of the Exodus.[1] "They have acted corruptly toward Him, they are not His children, because of their defect; But are a perverse and crooked generation [*genea* in the LXX]" (Deut. 32:5).[2]

DEFINING "THIS GENERATION"

Given the usage of the phrase "this generation" in the New Testament, this term should not be taken as a time frame reference in Matthew 24:34. Rather, it should be seen as a reference to a people group (certain Israelites) in a pejorative manner (they are disobedient and unbelieving). "This generation" is consistently referring to a people who refuse to trust and obey the words of God. In the immediate context of the Olivet Discourse, Jesus' words confirm that "this generation" transcends the first-century time frame. He accused "this generation" of killing Zechariah, an event that occurred hundreds of years earlier. The Jerusalem leadership embodied this type of person, and thus they received the rebuke of being "this generation," or unbelieving Israelites who oppose God's purposes. With this being the most compelling interpretation in Matthew 24:34, there are powerful theological points that arise from the Olivet Discourse.

THE EXPECTATION OF RESTORATION

To further define the usage of "this generation" in the Olivet Discourse, we must understand the expectation of the restoration of Israel and the crisis that a suffering Messiah presented to first-century Jews. Israel was sent into exile and Gentile domination at the time of the Babylon captivity because of their unfaithfulness to God. Although Israel has returned to the land several times, they still are under the discipline of God for unfaithfulness and unbelief. But God has promised that Israel will be restored. Israel will be obedient. The Messiah will come to Israel, and Israel will come to her Messiah. The prophets testify of this truth:

"For I will take you from the nations, gather you from all the lands and bring you into your own land. Then I will sprinkle clean water on you, and you will be clean; I will cleanse you from all your filthiness and from all your idols. Moreover, I will give you a new heart and put a new spirit within you; and I will remove the heart of stone from your flesh and give you a heart of flesh. I will put My Spirit within you and cause you to walk in My statutes, and you will be careful to observe My ordinances. You will live in the land that I gave to your forefathers; so you will be My people, and I will be your God. (Eze. 36:24–28)

"Also I will restore the captivity of My people Israel, and they will rebuild the ruined cities and live in them; they will also plant vineyards and drink their wine, and make gardens and eat their fruit. I will also plant them on their land, and they will not again be rooted out from their land which I have given them," says the Lord your God. (Amos 9:14–15)

The prophets testify that God will send His Messiah, who will crush the nations and save Israel. The prophets testify that the people of Israel, the natural descendants of Abraham, Isaac, and Jacob, will be purified by their God, planted in their own land, regenerated by the Holy Spirit, and obedient to all His statutes. This expectation was alive at the time of the coming of Christ. Roman occupation was loathed, and restoration was longed for. However, the people expected a conquering King, not a humble one. They expected Him to put to death the Roman occupation, not for Him to be put to death by them. But God's plans were greater. God sent His Son to proclaim the kingdom of God and to save not just Israel, but all the nations through His sacrifice. With this expectation as the backdrop, we can sketch the significance of "this generation."

The disciples were asking about "the end of the age." They surely associated the end of the age with the restoration of Israel. But not only was the Messiah going to suffer and die, but He was going to rise, ascend, and return. There was going to be a delay for an unknown amount of time in order for the gospel to go out to all the nations. Instead of the restoration of national Israel, their house was left desolate by their King. As a collective nation, they would not see their Messiah *until* they would say, "Blessed is He who comes in the name of the Lord" (Matt. 23:39). While there was going to be a delay, it was so that God would gather the constituency of His kingdom from every tribe, nation, and tongue. When this time is complete, all Israel will be saved.

> For I do not want you, brethren, to be uninformed of this mystery—so that you will not be wise in your own estimation— that a partial hardening has happened to Israel until the fullness of the Gentiles has come in; and so all Israel will be saved; just as it is written, "The Deliverer will come from Zion, He will remove

181

> ungodliness from Jacob. This is my
> covenant with them, when I take away
> their sins." (Rom. 11:25–26)

With this day fixed in the future, we can now see the significance of the profound statement that "this generation will not pass away until all these things take place."

"THIS GENERATION" *WILL* PASS AWAY

If we are consistent with Matthew's usage of this term—that "this generation" is a description of unbelieving Israel—then Jesus' proclamation explains what needs to take place before "this generation" (Israelites in unbelief) indeed passes away. All of the events Jesus outlined: false christs, wars, famines, the abomination of desolation, and the great persecution of God's elect must take place before all Israel is saved.

Recall that Jesus referenced the abomination of desolation, which is in the middle of the 70th seven. The prophecy of the 70 sevens was to answer Daniel's prayer regarding the destiny and restoration of His people, Israel. When the 70 sevens are fulfilled, then Israel will bring in "everlasting righteousness" (Dan. 9:24). The declaration that "this generation" will not pass away fits perfectly into the expectation of the end of the 70th seven. All of the things Jesus outlined must take place. These events take place prior to the completion of the 70th seven. Therefore, Israel as a people will be in partial unbelief until all these things take place. But when Jesus comes, He will remove ungodliness from Jacob, and they will look upon Him whom they pierced. As a nation, those who remain will believe at the completion of the 70th seven. At that time, there will be no Israelites who do not believe in Jesus of Nazareth. Thus, "this generation" will pass away. As a nation, the natural descendants of Abraham, Isaac, and Jacob will finally declare, "Blessed is He who comes in the name of the Lord."

End Notes 11

---

[1] Theologically, "this generation" could be seen as going all the way back to Cain. However, the term in its pejorative sense was first used in the scriptures to describe those of the Exodus who grumbled against the Lord.

[2] See Bob DeWaay, *This Generation and Its Preterist Exegetical Misuse*, CIC #100, June/July 2007, for further word studies on this term.

The Parable of the Fig Tree

12

A WORD OF COMFORT

Taking Solace in Our Sovereign Lord

Many reading this book may have their hearts struck with concern and worry. I confess that its contents contain many elements that may work anxiety in our minds. The prospect of having to endure the greatest persecution to ever occur is not a serene thought. This world is a battlefield. It is stained with sin and death. Most of its members are enemies of the Lord and His people. Yet, our great God recognizes our place and our plight and has given us strong encouragement to endure the path before us, whatever that may be. With all the points of this book that may cause us concern, in this chapter, through the Word of God, my desire is to impart comfort to those who are His chosen children.

"BLESSED ARE YOU"

Persecution is not something we desire, but it is something that is promised. Paul concludes that

185

"everyone wishing to live a godly life in Christ Jesus will be persecuted" (2 Tim. 3:12). Along with the gift of eternal life, we are also given the short-term reality of suffering. Again Paul states, "for it has been granted to you for Christ's sake, not only to believe in Him, but also to suffer for His sake" (Phil. 1:29). We must not make the mistake of thinking that persecution is somehow a sign that God is displeased with us. On the contrary, those who suffer for righteousness sake are considered blessed. Our Lord Himself proclaimed the blessedness of those who endure suffering for the sake of His gospel. In Matthew 5, we read:

> "Blessed are those who have been persecuted for the sake of righteousness, for theirs is the kingdom of heaven. Blessed are you when people insult you and persecute you, and falsely say all kinds of evil against you because of Me. Rejoice and be glad, for your reward in heaven is great; for in the same way they persecuted the prophets who were before you." (Matt. 5:10–12)

Those who are persecuted for the name of God are blessed. Even in the state of suffering, we can call upon the promises of God that will bring us comfort and hope. James calls us to remember Job:

> As an example, brethren, of suffering and patience, take the prophets who spoke in the name of the Lord. We count those blessed who endured. You have heard of the endurance of Job and have seen the

outcome of the Lord's dealings, that the
Lord is full of compassion and is merciful.
(James 5:10–11)

Persecution and suffering are promises for the
Christian. Those who endure suffering for the sake of
the gospel, in particular, are associated with the Lord
Himself. *That* is good company.

Linked with the Lord

When faced with opposition and suffering for the
truth, the Lord Himself told us to not be surprised
when the world aims its ire towards us.

> "If the world hates you, you know that it
> has hated Me before it hated you. If you
> were of the world, the world would love
> its own; but because you are not of the
> world, but I chose you out of the world,
> because of this the world hates you." (John
> 15:18–19)

While the world sees suffering as an
opportunity for mourning, the children of God are
called to rejoice when they suffer according to the will
of God.

> If you are reviled for the name of Christ,
> you are blessed, because the Spirit of glory
> and of God rests on you. Make sure that
> none of you suffers as a murderer, or thief,
> or evildoer, or a troublesome meddler; but
> if anyone suffers as a Christian, he is not to
> be ashamed, but is to glorify God in this
> name. (1 Pet. 5:14–16)

If the world treated the Lord of Hosts with contempt while He dwelt among us, we should not think we are above our Master. Rather, we can look to our Lord and have our hearts sing.

NOTHING CAN SEPARATE US

Whether we are in prosperity or want, health or sickness, peace or persecution, we need always to fix the eyes of our faith on the anchor of our souls. Though tribulation may threaten us to the point of losing our lives, we are called to rest in the truth that Christ has saved and secured us forever. The promises of God in Christ Jesus are our unfailing anchor, and we must hide these in our hearts. We must take strong hold of the encouragement that God has granted His chosen children.

> Who will separate us from the love of Christ? Will tribulation, or distress, or persecution, or famine, or nakedness, or peril, or sword? Just as it is written, "For your sake we are being put to death all day long; we were considered as sheep to be slaughtered." But in all these things we overwhelmingly conquer through Him who loved us. For I am convinced that neither death, nor life, nor angels, nor principalities, nor things present, nor things to come, nor powers, nor height, nor depth, nor any other created thing, will be able to separate us from the love of God, which is in Christ Jesus our Lord. (Rom. 8:35–39)

Let's take a closer look at the list that Paul declares cannot separate us from the love of God in Christ Jesus: tribulation, distress, persecution, famine, principalities, peril, and sword. All of these dangers have been highlighted throughout this book as intense realities of the time leading to the end of the age. Yet, nothing in all of creation has the ability to break the power of God's grip upon His children. This powerful passage will provide an unmovable anchor in the midst of life's ruinous storms.

THE WEIGHT OF GLORY

While the concerns and worries of this world may threaten to consume us, we are called to fix our hopes on the glory and grace that will come when Christ returns. In 2 Corinthians, Paul tells us the scales are heavily tipped in our favor.

> Therefore we do not lose heart, but though our outer man is decaying, yet our inner man is being renewed day by day. For momentary, light affliction is producing for us an eternal weight of glory far beyond all comparison, while we look not at the things which are seen, but at the things which are not seen; for the things which are seen are temporal, but the things which are not seen are eternal. (2 Cor. 4:16–18)

The troubles of this present age are light and momentary when compared to the weight of glory that awaits the redeemed. Even a "great tribulation" is unable to tip the scales. It is unworthy to be compared to the blessed, eternal state that awaits those who believe in Christ when He returns. If you believe in the person and work of Jesus of Nazareth, be encouraged! If you are persecuted for the name of Jesus Christ, count yourself blessed. Know that they treated the King in the same manner while He visited His creation. Since we are tethered to the powerful anchor that is our Great High Priest, let your heart rest in the knowledge that *nothing*—not tribulation, nor distress, nor persecution—can separate us from the love of God in Christ Jesus. We can rejoice in suffering, as Peter proclaimed:

> In this you greatly rejoice, even though now for a little while, if necessary, you have been distressed by various trials, so that the proof of your faith, being more precious than gold which is perishable, even though tested by fire, may be found to result in praise and glory and honor at the revelation of Jesus Christ. (1 Pet. 1:3–4)

We get a glimpse of the glory that awaits those who have a genuine faith. The Lord is preparing a place for us, and those who are His will reside with Him forever.

> I saw the holy city, new Jerusalem, coming down out of heaven from God, made ready as a bride adorned for her husband. And I heard a loud voice from the throne, saying, "Behold, the tabernacle of God is among men, and He will dwell among them, and they shall be His people, and God Himself

will be among them, and He will wipe away every tear from their eyes; and there will no longer be any death; there will no longer be any mourning, or crying, or pain; the first things have passed away." And He who sits on the throne said, "Behold, I am making all things new. "And He said, "Write, for these words are faithful and true." Then He said to me, "It is done. I am the Alpha and the Omega, the beginning and the end. I will give to the one who thirsts from the spring of the water of life without cost. He who overcomes will inherit these things, and I will be his God and he will be My son." (Rev. 21:2–7)

This is the eternal bliss that awaits those who overcome through the blood of the Lamb. So Christian, be comforted. The Lord is on your side.

THE PARABLE OF THE FIG TREE

13

WATCH AND PRAY

Putting the Parable of the Fig Tree into Practice

"Therefore everyone who hears these words of Mine and acts on them, may be compared to a wise man who built his house on the rock. And the rain fell, and the floods came, and the winds blew and slammed against that house; and yet it did not fall, for it had been founded on the rock. Everyone who hears these words of Mine and does not act on them, will be like a foolish man who built his house on the sand. The rain fell, and the floods came, and the winds blew and slammed against that house; and it fell—and great was its fall." (Matt. 7:24–27)

These powerful words of Christ, spoken in the wake of the Sermon on the Mount, have a very practical implication for us today. We can study diligently and discover the meaning of end-times passages. We can construct all sorts of charts and graphs. We can be razor sharp in our exposition. Yet, if we fail to put what we learn into practice, we are deceiving ourselves. Note James' wisdom:

> But prove yourselves doers of the word, and not merely hearers who delude themselves. (James 1:22)

Jesus has instructed us to learn the parable of the fig tree. This simple and profound parable gives us insight into the dynamics of the end of the age. It is imperative that we put its lessons into practice. For those who believe in Christ and trust His Word, our marching orders come from Him. The way we put the parable of the fig tree into practice is to watch and pray.

WATCH!

There are two related, but distinct dynamics regarding "watching" for the return of Christ. The first is clear from the parable of the fig tree. We are to watch for the signs of the times. If the figurative fig tree begins to bud—if the signs heralding His return sprout on the scene of human history—then we are to know that He is near. We are to stand watch, and only when the clear indicators given to us by our Lord begin to transpire are we to blow the horn that His coming is "right at the doors."

Yet, being on the alert for the signs of the end is only part of watching. After Jesus told us "everything in advance," He proceeded to give us two powerful parables. These parables contrast one another so we don't fall into improper action while we are waiting.

194

They teach us how we need to "watch ourselves" in our walk with the Lord until He returns.

The Parable of the Ten Virgins

The first parable in Matthew 25 is the parable of the virgins. Following is the parable in its entirety:

> "Then the kingdom of heaven will be comparable to ten virgins, who took their lamps and went out to meet the bridegroom. Five of them were foolish, and five were prudent. For when the foolish took their lamps, they took no oil with them, but the prudent took oil in flasks along with their lamps. Now while the bridegroom was delaying, they all got drowsy and began to sleep. But at midnight there was a shout, 'Behold, the bridegroom! Come out to meet him. Then all those virgins rose and trimmed their lamps. The foolish said to the prudent, 'Give us some of your oil, for our lamps are going out.' But the prudent answered, 'No, there will not be enough for us and you too; go instead to the dealers and buy some for yourselves.' And while they were going away to make the purchase, the bridegroom came, and those who were ready went in with him to the wedding feast; and the door was shut. Later the other virgins also came, saying, 'Lord, lord, open up for us. But he answered, 'Truly I say to you, I do not know you.' Be on the

alert then, for you do not know the day nor
the hour." (Matt. 25:1–13)

Understanding the first century wedding
ceremony is essential to understanding this parable.
The dynamics of a first century wedding feast were as
follows: When all the preparations for both the
marriage and the feast were complete, the groom
would go to retrieve his bride. Depending upon where
the bride was, this might have taken some time, and
the groom might have been delayed. Once the bride
joined the groom, a processional began heading to
where the feast was held. Along the way, young virgin
ladies would often join the processional with lamps,
helping to light the way. Once they arrived at the
house of the banquet, all would then enter the feast
for a time of celebration.[1]

Notice, Jesus begins this parable declaring "at
that time," meaning at the time of the coming of the
Son of Man described in Matthew 24:30–36, the
kingdom of heaven will be compared to the point of
this parable.

First, note that the virgins were "sleeping"
because the bridegroom took longer than expected.
Contrary to other end-times teachings, in this text,
"sleeping" is not negative. It simply highlights the fact
of the bridegroom's delay. Both the wise and the
foolish were sleeping. Second, the wise took extra oil.
They were prepared for a delay. They were ready.
Their wisdom and prudence were evident before the
bridegroom arrived so that when he did, even if he
were delayed, they could join the processional and

enter the feast with him. Third, the shocking response to those who are unprepared is, *"I do not know you!"* Those who were not wise and did not bring extra oil were unable to enter the feast. Because they did not prepare for the delay, they missed the processional and the door to the feast was shut.

WHAT DOES THE OIL SIGNIFY?

Numerous suggestions have been offered as to what the oil in this parable signifies. Again, we must be careful to not go beyond the intent of the parable. The point is explicitly stated by Christ: "Be on the alert then, for you do not know the day nor the hour" (25:13). Since we do not know the day or the hour, it may take longer than we think. Therefore, we must always be on the alert. The extra oil certainly indicates proper preparation and wisdom as one waits for the bridegroom.

If there is another layer to the significance to the oil, it may well represent the expectation of Christ's return. The foolish virgin's lamps were going dim. They were not prepared for the delay. The wise virgins had extra oil to keep their lamps burning. They were prepared, and when the bridegroom arrived, they proceeded with Him to the feast. An exhortation in the book of Luke undergirds this conclusion. In a distinct yet related parable, Jesus declares, "Be dressed in readiness, and keep your lamps lit. Be like men who are waiting for their master when he returns from the wedding feast, so that they may immediately open the door to him when he comes and knocks" (Luke 12:35–36). The command requires constant readiness and expectation.

How a "Delay" Should Sober Us

In Matthew 25, there are several indicators of a delay before the return of Jesus Christ.

Note these examples:

> "Now while the bridegroom *was delaying*, they all got drowsy and began to sleep." (Matt. 25:5, emphasis added)

> "Now *after a long time* the master of those slaves came and settled accounts with them." (Matt. 25:19, emphasis added)

Furthermore, James exhorts us to be patient as we wait.

> Therefore be patient, brethren, until the coming of the Lord. The farmer waits for the precious produce of the soil, being patient about it, until it gets the early and late rains. You too be patient. (James 5:7–8)

Why do the Spirit-led authors of scripture stress this point of delay and exhort patience in light of it? In the midst of great expectation, delay can be disheartening. If an attitude of impatience and disbelief begin to take root, danger looms. As we have seen, Jesus exhorts His people to always be alert, prepared, and laboring. These qualities are necessary to keep our expectations high because our sinful hearts can easily be drawn away by the deceitfulness of this world. We don't know the day or the hour. He may come sooner than we think. Or He may delay. Both of these possibilities demand our utmost devotion to our King so that, when He does come, by His grace we may hear, "Well done, good and faithful servant. Enter into the joy of your Master."

If we apply Christ's parable to His plain teaching in the Olivet Discourse, the wise are those who watched and heeded Christ's commands to not lose their hope and expectation *even if the Lord delays*. The wise virgins were prepared to meet their Master. They were continually ready, not succumbing to the world's deception. When He comes, they will enter the feast. The foolish are those who were not prepared for the delay. They are shocked when the bridegroom comes and find no way to join the joy that His coming brings to those who trust Him. Only those who are prepared will enter the feast. Those who aren't will be shut out.

How does this parable speak to our preparation? The point is utterly uncomplicated. We are to be continually "ready and wise." From our perspective, we see there already has been a delay—two thousand years. But one day there will be an announcement, "Here comes the bridegroom!" Will we be wise and ready? Only those who are Christ's will join that processional to the sky. We must watch and pray. We don't know when the appointed time will come. Jesus' final direct words of exhortation in the Olivet Discourse, then, make perfect sense. "Be on the alert then, for you do not know the day nor the hour" (25:13).

While we wait, we must be watching, vigilant, patient, and prepared. If we do not have the expectation of Christ returning, we risk becoming dull of hearing, prey to deception, and that day may come upon us like a trap. Through the Holy Spirit, we must constantly guard our hearts from the deceitfulness of sin. Remember, the Lord has the ability to blind our eyes to what is going on. If we become conformed to this world, we will cease watching and become susceptible to Satan's schemes. Hear Jesus' instruction in Luke regarding our need for constant watchfulness:

> "Be on guard, so that your hearts will not be weighted down with dissipation and drunkenness and the worries of life, and that day will not come on you suddenly like a trap; for it will come upon all those who dwell on the face of all the earth. (Luke 21:34–35)

So we must carefully watch ourselves, our beliefs, and our practices. To further build upon what we should be doing as we await Christ's return, He grants us a parable that calls us to labor while the harvest is still at hand.

THE PARABLE OF THE TALENTS

On the heels of the parable of the ten virgins, Jesus gave us the parable of the talents. The parable reads as follows:

"For it is just like a man about to go on a journey, who called his own slaves and entrusted his possessions to them. To one he gave five talents, to another, two, and to another, one, each according to his own ability; and he went on his journey. Immediately the one who had received the five talents went and traded with them, and gained five more talents. In the same manner the one who had received the two talents gained two more. But he who received the one talent went away, and dug a hole in the ground and hid his master's money. Now after a long time the master of those slaves came and settled accounts with them. The one who had received the five talents came up and brought five more talents, saying, 'Master, you entrusted five talents to me. See, I have gained five more talents.' His master said to him, 'Well done, good and faithful slave You were faithful with a few things, I will put you in charge of many things; enter into the joy of your master.' Also the one who had received the two talents came up and said, 'Master, you entrusted two talents to me. See, I have gained two more talents.' His master said to him, 'Well done, good and faithful slave. You were faithful with a few things, I will put you in charge of many things; enter into the joy of your master.' And the one also who had received the one talent came up and said, 'Master, I knew you to be a hard

man, reaping where you did not sow and
gathering where you scattered no seed.
And I was afraid, and went away and hid
your talent in the ground. See, you have
what is yours.' But his master answered
and said to him, 'You wicked, lazy slave,
you knew that I reap where I did not sow
and gather where I scattered no seed.
Then you ought to have put my money in
the bank, and on my arrival I would have
received my money back with interest.
Therefore take away the talent from him,
and give it to the one who has the ten
talents.' For to everyone who has, more
shall be given, and he will have an
abundance; but from the one who does not
have, even what he does have shall be
taken away. Throw out the worthless
slave into the outer darkness; in that place
there will be weeping and gnashing of
teeth." (Matt. 25:14–30)

A talent was a unit of currency. In this parable,
the elements are fairly self-evident. Before the master
goes away, he gives four servants a portion of his
property. Each is entrusted with a different amount.
Three were faithful and wise, investing the talents and
making a profit. These servants are commended and
enter into their master's joy when he returns. The last
servant, however, hid his talent and received his
master's rage: "You wicked and slothful servant!"

This parable highlights the immense importance of
laboring with whatever our Master has granted. While
we await His return, we must be working hard with

what He has given us. Whether the gifts be spiritual or physical, all are to be used for the glory of the King. The advance of the gospel and the glorification of Jesus Christ is the primary task of His church. Therefore, we must heed this parable admonishing us to not "bury" ourselves and our gifts, but rather strive to be fruitful in good works for the gospel.

It is easy to slip into a survivalist mentality when envisioning the end of the age. We must resist this leaning. First and foremost, we are to be laboring in love for the advance of the kingdom of God through the gospel. We are to be administering our spiritual gifts to those in the body of Christ and thus be pleasing to our Master.

In order to be "faithful watchers" as these two parables teach, we must also incorporate a primary command of Christ: *Pray.*

Pray!

In the conclusion of Luke's end-times discourse, Jesus' words of exhortation provide the climax of His teaching.

> "But keep on the alert at all times, praying
> that you may have strength to escape all
> these things that are about to take place,
> and to stand before the Son of Man."
> (Luke 21:36)

In the midst of watching, we are to be constantly asking God for "strength to escape" all that is about to come to pass. This is a command from our

King: *pray at all times.* We must not wait for the signs of the end to begin praying for strength from on High. It needs to begin now. Whatever may come to pass, we need to pray to the God of all grace to sustain our hearts. Though the fires of temptation and suffering may test our faith, we must look to Him for the power to escape through the fire. The word "escape" in this text points to process of coming through the fires of temptation and trials unscathed by disobedience.

Our prayer is that when He returns, we would be able "to stand" before the Son of Man. This hearkens back to the point of continually expecting the return of Christ. We are to keep this day fixed in our hearts. He is our Lord and Master. We know that one day we will be brought before Him to give account. But will we be able to *stand*? To "stand" is the position of one who has faithfully passed the test and not succumbed to the seduction of this world and its principles. In this context, those who will "stand" before the Son of Man are the ones who faithfully navigate the end of the age and arrive before their King as faithful servants. Therefore, we are called to always pray for the strength to escape all that is about to come to pass and to stand before the Son of Man.

How will we have the strength to stand? We do not stand in our own strength or power. We well remember, as the doxology at the end of the book of Jude declares, that it is only in the Savior's power that we stand.

Now to Him who is able to keep you from stumbling, and *to make you stand* in the presence of His glory blameless with great joy, to the only God our Savior, through Jesus Christ our Lord, be glory, majesty, dominion and authority, before all time and now and forever. Amen. (Jude 24–25, emphasis added)

PRAY FOR BOLDNESS

We are equipped with every spiritual blessing in Jesus Christ. In His grace, God has given us everything pertaining to life and godliness. Our cups runneth over. Yet, even though the Spirit of the living God resides in those who believe, this does not negate the need for prayer. In fact, the reality that the Spirit resides in us ought to fuel us to go before the throne of grace. Since it is the message of the gospel that is the advancing force of His kingdom, we need to pray for boldness to open our mouths and announce the only message that can save humans from their sins. This is our duty as ambassadors of Jesus Christ. We are called to venture into the world and plead with them to be reconciled to God. Consider Paul's teaching in 2 Corinthians 5:

Now all these things are from God, who reconciled us to Himself through Christ and gave us the ministry of reconciliation, namely, that God was in Christ reconciling the world to Himself, not counting their trespasses against them, and He has committed to us the word of

205

> reconciliation. Therefore, we are
> ambassadors for Christ, as though God
> were making an appeal through us; we
> beg you on behalf of Christ, be reconciled
> to God. (2 Cor. 5:18–20)

Since we are given this enormous responsibility, we cannot allow the notion of self-sufficiency to fill our minds. We are finite. We are frail. We are weak. We need power from on High to fulfill this calling. Though we indeed have the Holy Spirit of God as our advocate and helper, we still are taught to continually pray for confidence to announce His glories and gospel to a dying world. Consider the example of the early church. The Spirit had just been poured out and, in typical form, persecution immediately followed. When the church gathered, they prayed the following petition:

> "And now, Lord, take note of their
> threats, and grant that Your bond-servants
> may speak Your word with all
> confidence." (Acts 4:29)

Furthermore, the apostle Paul recognized the need for prayer to proclaim the gospel with boldness.

> Pray on my behalf, that utterance may be
> given to me in the opening of my mouth, to
> make known with boldness the mystery of
> the gospel, for which I am an ambassador
> in chains; that in proclaiming it I may
> speak boldly, as I ought to speak. (Eph.
> 6:19–20)

Prayer is an indispensable part of preparation for the end of the age. We are to pray for the strength to endure the fires of tribulation that we may encounter. We are to pray for the power to proclaim the word of the gospel with conviction and boldness. We are to pray for the name of our King to be magnified. In doing this now, by God's grace, we are well equipped to endure the rough terrain that lays before us.

SOBERING WORDS FROM OUR COMMANDING OFFICER

The tone and teaching of Jesus in reference to the time of the end should cause us to wake up. These are not trivial matters. These are words that should awaken us to the fact that we live in a time of war in which the dangers are escalating. The stakes couldn't be higher. The souls of our friends, our families, and our own selves are in the midst of a raging battle. We only see a small portion of that war, but we are to make no mistake. We are in the middle of a cosmic conflict that stretches back to the beginning.

> For our struggle is not against flesh and blood, but against the rulers, against the powers, against the world forces of this darkness, against the spiritual forces of wickedness in the heavenly places. (Eph. 6:12)

With this as our unseen reality, we need to open and understand the scripture's "call to arms." To this immensely important point we now proceed.

End Notes 13

---

[1] See Kenneth E. Bailey, *Jesus Through Middle Eastern Eyes* (Downers Grove: Intervarsity Press, 2008), 269-275.

14

A CALL TO ARMS

Becoming Battle Ready for the "Evil Day"

*E*ndure. This command resounds throughout the scriptures. Those who are called into service for the King of Kings are to endure hardship. Paul exhorts Timothy (and by implication all of us) in this way: "You therefore must endure hardship as a good soldier of Jesus Christ. No one engaged in warfare entangles himself with the affairs of this life, that he may please him who enlisted him as a soldier" (2 Tim. 2:3–4). The call is clear. We are soldiers who need to stand. We need to patiently endure the persecution and trials that are aimed our way. In Ephesians 6, the apostle Paul gives a call to arms. The Christian is called to put on the full armor of God.

> Be strong in the Lord and in the strength of His might. Put on the full armor of God, so that you will be able to stand firm against the schemes of the devil. (Eph. 6:10–11)

There are six pieces that constitute the "full armor of God." This figurative battle gear is how Christ has called His people to prepare for the spiritual war that rages. Paul utilizes the typical armor of a Roman soldier as an illustration to exhort believers to position themselves on the battle lines.

> Stand firm therefore, having girded your loins with truth, and having put on the breastplate of righteousness, and having shod your feet with the preparation of the gospel of peace; in addition to all, taking up the shield of faith with which you will be able to extinguish all the flaming arrows of the evil one. And take the helmet of salvation, and the sword of the Spirit, which is the word of God. (Eph. 6:14–17)

First we are to fasten *the belt of truth*. This was the first piece of armor to which much of the other armor attached. Next the *breastplate of righteousness* is placed over the shoulders to protect all the vital organs. Then we are to take up the *shield of faith*, which can extinguish all the flaming darts of the evil one. Enemy soldiers would often light their arrows, which would ignite the shield and force one to abandon their protection. The shield of faith is able not only to stop the flaming arrow but to extinguish it, as well. Then we are to put on the *helmet of salvation*. The helmet was indispensable, as it protected the head from any attack launched by the enemy. Finally, we are to pick up the *sword of the Spirit*, which is the Word of God. Properly utilizing the scriptures will provide a strong defense, able to deflect the most serious attack, but also serving as an unstoppable offensive weapon.

We need to view all of the above pieces as parts of a whole. They poetically describe our position in Christ while we stand firm on the foreign soil of this world. All of the pieces of armor also point to the person and work of Jesus Christ. He is the *truth* (John 14:6). He is our *righteousness* (1 Cor. 1:30) . He has produced the *peace* (Eph. 2:4) by which we stand through the gospel. He is the object, author, and finisher of our *faith* (Heb. 12:2). He is the source of our *salvation* (Acts 4:12). He is the *Word of God* incarnate (John 1:14). We are exhorted to continually put on this armor. This is the apostle Paul's poetic manner of commanding us to abide in the wondrous work and powerful person of Jesus Christ. We have everything we need in Jesus Christ. Therefore, let us stand firm in His salvific and sustaining power.

Why Do We Need to Put on the Full Armor?

Why are we commanded to put on the full armor of God? Why must we be reminded to abide the person and perfect work of Jesus Christ? Because we have a roaring enemy who seeks to devour us. Spiritual evil is unseen, but all too real.

> For our struggle is not against flesh and blood, but against the rulers, against the powers, against the world forces of this darkness, against the spiritual forces of

211

wickedness in the heavenly places.
Therefore, take up the full armor of God,
so that you will be able to resist in the evil day,
and having done everything, to stand firm.
(Eph. 6:12–13, emphasis added)

Since our battle is ultimately against the
principalities and powers opposed to our God and His
purposes, we need His power in order that we may
stand in the "evil day." The term "evil day" may refer
to any trial that the believer may encounter. But there
is a definite article that precedes the term, which may
indicate (and certainly includes) the ultimate "evil day"
that will occur when "a great tribulation, such as
never has occurred nor ever will again" transpires. We
need His power to stand through all of the threats
that constitute the time of the end.

PREPARING FOR THE THREE-PRONGED THREAT

The cosmic battle that has been raging since the
Garden of Eden will come to a crescendo at the end of
the age. Whoever you are and wherever you live, at
that time threats will close in on all sides. Three
primary threats will preside: *persecution, deception,* and
divine wrath. In the following section, I want us to
hear the preparatory exhortations for these dangers
that will be unleashed at the end of the age but that
are already in our midst.

BE PREPARED FOR PERSECUTION

Much of the Christian world already knows the painful reality of persecution. Every year, multitudes give their lives because of their confession of Christ. Even more are hated and mistreated because of their stand for the Savior. Others are not well acquainted with such persecution. Many live in conditions that are calm compared to what their brethren are experiencing. We must always remember to pray for our spiritual siblings who are suffering for the gospel. We, ourselves, must prepare our minds with a proper scriptural outlook should such we encounter such a time.

The first point of preparation upon which we need to fix in our minds is not being surprised when we or others suffer for the gospel. When we believe the gospel, we are not given a life free from suffering. On the contrary, we are promised persecution.

> Indeed, all who desire to live godly in Christ Jesus will be persecuted. (2 Tim. 3:12)

When the tide of tribulation begins to rise, we may well become anxious and full of worry. In extreme tribulation, believers may be asking, "What will I eat? What will I wear? What will happen to my loved ones?" Such questions are natural, but our Lord tells us to rest in the Father's care.

> Do not seek what you will eat and what you will drink, and do not keep worrying. For all these things the nations of the

> world eagerly seek; but your Father knows
> that you need these things. But seek His
> kingdom, and these things will be added
> to you. (Luke 12:28–31)

If believers find themselves in such persecution that they are called before authorities, the questions may become even more pressing. "What if I deny my Lord?" This anxiety has plagued persecuted believers since the early church. Once again, our active call is to offer our anxieties up to the Father.

> Be anxious for nothing, but in everything
> by prayer and supplication with
> thanksgiving let your requests be made
> known to God. And the peace of God,
> which surpasses all comprehension, will
> guard your hearts and your minds in Christ
> Jesus. (Phil. 4:6–7)

Beyond this, we are commanded not to worry even about what we will say. If left to ourselves, we would certainly fail. But Christ has given us the Comforter. The Holy Spirit abides in every believer, and the Lord gives us the following instructions if we are persecuted to such an extent.

> "When they bring you before the
> synagogues and the rulers and the
> authorities, do not worry about how or
> what you are to speak in your defense, or
> what you are to say; for the Holy Spirit
> will teach you in that very hour what you
> ought to say." (Luke 12:11–12)

So we are not to even worry about what we will say if we are called before ungodly authorities. The Holy Spirit will give us the words that very hour. Since the Holy Spirit testifies to the person and work of Jesus Christ, we should stand firm and trust His Word that He will give us words and we will not fail when called to the test.

During the Nazi Holocaust, a Dutch Christian woman named Corrie ten Boom put her life on the line to preserve the natural descendants of Abraham, Isaac, and Jacob. Eventually, she was betrayed and sent to a concentration camp. There she testified of the grace of Jesus Christ and stood firm in His gospel. Though she faithfully endured intense tribulation, she recognized that an even greater trial for all of God's people lay on the horizon of human history. This prophetic voice from the past speaks to the reality of the present and the future.

> In China, the Christians were told, "Don't worry, before the tribulation comes you will be translated—raptured." Then came a terrible persecution. Millions of Christians were tortured to death. Later I heard a Bishop from China say sadly, "We have failed. We should have made the people strong for persecution rather than telling them Jesus would come first. Tell the people how to be strong in times of persecution, how to stand when the tribulation comes—to stand and not faint."
>
> I feel I have a divine mandate to go and tell the people of this world that it is

possible to be strong in the Lord Jesus Christ. We are in training for the tribulation, but more than 60 percent of the Body of Christ across the world has already entered into the tribulation. There is no way to escape it. We are next.

Since I have already gone through prison for Jesus' sake, and since I met the Bishop in China, now every time I read a good Bible text I think, "Hey, I can use that in the time of tribulation." Then I write it down and learn it by heart. When I was in the concentration camp, a camp where only twenty percent of the women came out alive, we tried to cheer each other up by saying, "Nothing could be any worse than today." But we would find the next day was even worse. During this time a Bible verse that I had committed to memory gave me great hope and joy. "If ye be reproached for the name of Christ, happy are ye; for the spirit of glory and of God resteth upon you; on their part evil is spoken of, but on your part He is glorified" (1 Pet. 3:14). I found myself saying, "Hallelujah! Because I am suffering, Jesus is glorified!"[1]

Therefore, may we hide the Word of God in our hearts, pray without ceasing, and trust that the Lord will preserve us if we are called to be the people who endure persecution, especially a persecution without equal. This is how we prepare for such.

Be Ready to Deflect Deception

As made plain in all the major end-times texts, deception is unleashed just prior to the end of the age. The Spirit-led authors of the scriptures to concur.

> "For false christs and false prophets will arise and will show great signs and wonders, so as to mislead, if possible, even the elect." (Matt. 24:24)

> . . . That is, the one whose coming is in accord with the activity of Satan, with all power and signs and false wonders, and with all the deception of wickedness for those who perish, because they did not receive the love of the truth so as to be saved. (2 Thess. 2:9–10)

> And he deceives those who dwell on the earth because of the signs which it was given him to perform in the presence of the beast. (Rev. 13:14)

If we are to be well prepared to deflect deception, we need to become well trained in wielding the sword of the Spirit, the Word of God. Training needs to begin now. We don't know when the appointed time will come. Because of this, we must take action immediately. If we do not hear and abide in the words of Christ, we will fall prey to deception. We need our senses trained by the Word of God to be able to detect and avoid evil. Through diligently reading, understanding, and applying the scripture, our swords become sharpened and our skill becomes greater.

Since the deception at the end of the age will be so intense, our need is to become expert swordsmen. This takes time, energy, and practice. But for those who become well acquainted with the Word and how to properly apply it, we will be ready to deflect deception for both the present and the time to come.

Know You Are Delivered from Divine Wrath

The ultimate threat of the end of the age is not tribulation or deception itself. It is that one falls prey to these things and aligns oneself against the Lord of Hosts. The wrath of God is real and will be unleashed upon this world as never before. We should not fear what humans can do in comparison to God. Jesus told us whom we should fear.

> "I say to you, My friends, do not be afraid of those who kill the body and after that have no more that they can do. But I will warn you whom to fear: fear the One who, after He has killed, has authority to cast into hell; yes, I tell you, fear Him!" (Luke 12:4–5)

If you have not believed in the person and work of Jesus Christ—His sinless life, His atoning death on the cross, His resurrection, and promised return—then I plead with you. Repent (which means to turn from sin and self) and believe (which means to trust in the person, words, and the work of Jesus) and you will not be destined for wrath.

Again, Paul proclaims the promise:

> For God has not destined us for wrath, but
> for obtaining salvation through our Lord
> Jesus Christ. (1 Thess. 5:9)

This wrath includes the Day of the Lord, which will crush the nations and its inhabitants at the end of the age. It also includes His eternal wrath, which will forever be the reality of those who do not obey the gospel of Jesus Christ (2 Thess. 1:11). We who repent and believe have a promise: that Jesus will deliver us from the wrath of God. Paul tells believers, "You turned to God from idols to serve a living and true God, and to wait for His Son from heaven, whom He raised from the dead, that is Jesus, who rescues us from the wrath to come" (1 Thess. 1:9–10).

MUSTERING THE TROOPS

Thus we wait. We endure. All who believe in Jesus Christ have been born of God, and as His children, it is our birthright to rest in the knowledge that Jesus has delivered us from the coming wrath. Our Lord asks a sobering question regarding His return.

> "Will not God bring about justice for His
> elect who cry to Him day and night, and
> will He delay long over them? I tell you
> that He will bring about justice for them
> quickly. However, when the Son of Man
> comes, will He find faith on the earth?"
> (Luke 18:7–8)

May the Holy Spirit muster the troops of Jesus Christ so that He does find faith when He comes. The war is already being waged, and it will only escalate as we approach the end. As "good soldiers of Jesus Christ," may the remnant be roused to endure hardship with the hope-filled message of the gospel set firmly in our souls. Let us heed the call to arms echoed in the pages of scripture. Grip tightly the sword of the Spirit, which is the Word of God, as it will deflect deception. Pick up the powerful activity of prayer, as it is essential to our stance of watching. Finally, may we not neglect gathering together as the fellowship of the called out ones, but rather "encourage one another all the more as we see that day drawing near" (Heb. 10:25).

The Father has fixed the day of His Son's glorious return. We have that "day and hour" withheld from us. Yet, our Savior has graciously given us powerful words of preparation. Being fully equipped by His establishing grace, let us stand firm on the "walls of the watchmen" as we wait for our conquering King to deliver us.

End Notes 14

---

[1] From "Prepared for the Coming Tribulation," a letter written by Corrie ten Boom in 1974. This letter was verified as authentic in a personal interview with Pastor Anton Verdam, who has served in Amsterdam and worked closely with those associated with Corrie ten Boom and her ministry.

The Parable of the Fig Tree

March 11, 2009

Jerusalem

REFLECTIONS FROM
THE MOUNT OF OLIVES

In His providence, the Lord has given me the privilege of finishing this book in the city of Jerusalem. It is humbling to be putting the finishing strokes on this work while sitting on the Mount of Olives, the very place where Jesus gave His great end-times discourse, the very mount where He ascended, and the awesome place we were given the promise that this same Jesus would come again.

From this vantage point, we can view a vast panorama of the city of Jerusalem. This city is described in the scriptures as "a cup of trembling" (Zech. 12:2). I can see the Temple Mount from where I sit. One day, that site will be the epicenter of a tribulation that will echo throughout the world.

It is springtime here in Israel. The fig trees are budding. Summer is near. We do not know the times

223

and the seasons that our Lord has set. Yet, we are called to recognize the time of the end when the events He revealed to us begin to unfold.

We know our King is risen. We know He has ascended and is seated at the right hand of the Father. We know that He is returning to rescue us and raise us to life everlasting. As we eagerly await this day, may we all stand girded with the gospel of grace. The exhortation He gave to His disciples on this very mount in the first century we must heed today:

> "What I say to you, I say to all: *'Watch.'*"(Mark 13:37 NKJV, emphasis added)

ABOUT THE AUTHOR

Ryan Habbena is the pastor of preaching and teaching at Conquering King Fellowship in St. Paul, Minnesota. He is also the director of Signet Ring Ministries, a biblical teaching and resource ministry. Ryan holds two degrees in Biblical and Theological studies (B.A. Bethel University, M.A. Bethel Seminary [New Testament]). Ryan lives with his wife and three children just outside of St. Paul, MN.

For more resources from the
ministry of Ryan Habbena, go to:

SIGNET R✝NG
MINISTRIES

www.signetringministries.org

CONQUERING
K✝NG
FELLOWSHIP

www.ckfellowship.org